Valerie

DRESSMAKING
SIMPLIFIED

Third Edition

OXFORD

BLACKWELL SCIENTIFIC PUBLICATIONS

LONDON EDINBURGH BOSTON

MELBOURNE PARIS BERLIN VIENNA

Blackwell Scientific Publications
Editorial offices:
Osney Mead, Oxford OX2 0EL
25 John Street, London WC1N 2BL
23 Ainslie Place, Edinburgh EH3 6AJ
238 Main Street, Cambridge
    MA 02142, USA
54 University Street, Carlton
    Victoria 3053, Australia

Other Editorial Offices:
Librairie Arnette SA
2, rue Casimir-Delavigne
75006 Paris
France

Blackwell Wissenschafts-Verlag
Meinekestrasse 4
D-1000 Berlin 15
Germany

Blackwell MZV
Feldgasse 13
A-1238 Wien
Austria

First published in Great Britain by
    MacGibbon & Kee Ltd 1971
Second edition (metric) published by
    Crosby Lockwood Staples 1976
Reprinted 1977
Third edition published by
    Granada Publishing 1981
Reprinted in paperback 1984
Reprinted by Collins Professional and
    Technical Books 1985
Reprinted by BSP Professional Books
    1988, 1990, 1991, 1992
Reprinted by Blackwell Scientific
    Publications 1992

Set by V&M Graphics Ltd, Aylesbury
Printed and bound in Great Britain by
    Hollen Street Press Ltd,
    Slough, Berkshire

DISTRIBUTORS

Marston Book Services Ltd
PO Box 87
Oxford OX2 0DT
(*Orders:* Tel: 0865 791155
        Fax: 0865 791927
        Telex: 837515)

USA
    Blackwell Scientific Publications, Inc.
    238 Main Street
    Cambridge, MA 02142
    (*Orders:* Tel: (800) 759–6102
            (617) 225–0401)

Canada
    Oxford University Press
    70 Wynford Drive
    Don Mills
    Ontario M3C 1J9
    (*Orders:* Tel: (416) 441–2941)

Australia
    Blackwell Scientific Publications
    (Australia) Pty Ltd
    54 University Street
    Carlton, Victoria 3053
    (*Orders:* Tel: (03) 347–0300)

British Library
Cataloguing in Publication Data

Cock, Valerie I.
Dressmaking simplified. – 3rd ed.
    1. Women's clothing. Making –
    Manuals
I. Title
646 4'04

ISBN 0–632–02216–7

CONTENTS

1 EQUIPMENT

2 FABRIC FIBRES AND THEIR SOURCE

3 PERSONAL APPEARANCE

4 TAKING MEASUREMENTS

5 PATTERN ALTERATION

Contents

6 CONSTRUCTION OF A GARMENT

7 DISPOSAL OF FULLNESS

8 SEAMS

Contents

Contents

Contents

ACKNOWLEDGEMENT

The author would like to express her thanks to Miss Margaret Humfrey for all her help with the general organization of this book and the revision of the typescript.

KEY TO ABBREVIATIONS

↓ ↓ ↓	Tailor Tacks
————— — ————— — —————	Fitting Line
—— —— —— ——	Tacked Line
— — — — — — — —	Machine Stitched Line
R.S.	Right Side
W.S.	Wrong Side
C.F.	Centre Front
C.B.	Centre Back
Diag.	Diagram

1 EQUIPMENT

To obtain good results it is necessary to use the correct equipment and to ensure that all tools are kept in good working order. Do not misuse tools: for example, fine scissors should not be used for cutting string, paper or thick fabrics.

General Equipment

Table: This must be firm enough to support the sewing machine which vibrates in use. It should, if possible, be at least 54 inches wide, for ease when cutting out; and sufficiently large to hold the garment being made and the tools in use.

Mirror: Full length for fitting and deciding hem length, also for the appreciation of style, colour and fabrics.

Iron and Pressing equipment: see page 16.

Box or Container: For storing the garment whilst under construction.

Hanging Space: For partly finished garments.

Cupboard or Drawer Space: For sewing equipment.

Tissue Paper: For care of white fabrics and those which crease easily. Tissue paper is also used to support seams which are to be machine-stitched on very fine fabrics such as chiffon.

Dressmaking Simplified

Sewing Equipment

Scissors: Three pairs are necessary.

Cutting out scissors: 21 to 23 cm long with one narrow pointed blade and one wider, heavier blade with one larger handle for the fingers.

Medium pair: 13 to 16 cm long with narrow pointed blades to be used for trimming seams and general use.

Both pairs should be kept well sharpened.

An old pair of scissors for cutting paper and thick thread.

Pins: Use steel dressmaker pins; these are slender and well pointed. Brass pins are coarse and tend to leave black marks. For fine fabrics which mark easily, use fine crewel needles. Discard *all* rusty pins.

Thimble: A steel thimble is best as this metal is very strong: check that the surface is smooth as rough areas harm fine fabrics. Solid silver thimbles are too soft for constant use. Plastic thimbles crack easily.

Tape Measure: Choose a strong, clearly marked measure with metal ends. If possible, with one end being rigid for 5–8 cm for help in turning hems, etc. A limp measure is apt to stretch and become inaccurate.

Ruler: If transparent and flexible, generally useful.

Yardstick: Used for pattern alterations, cutting out and marking hem lines.

Tailor's Chalk: Brushes off easily: can be used for marking hem lines and alterations.

Carbon Paper: Available in colours; marks wash out easily; used for transferring pattern markings and designs.

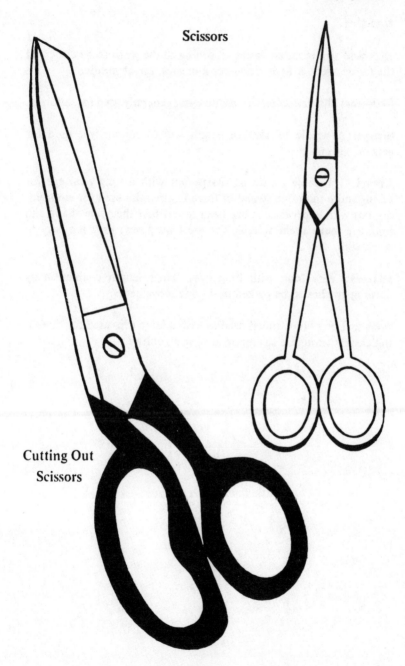

Equipment

Scissors

Cutting Out
Scissors

Dressmaking Simplified

Needles

Type and size required varies according to the work to be done and the fabric used. A higher number indicates a finer needle.

Betweens: Short needles with round eyes; generally used for tailoring.

Sharps: A needle of average length with a round eye; used for general sewing.

Crewel: The same length as sharps but with a long oval eye for taking more than one strand of thread; generally used for embroidery but with experience it has been found that their fine shape and long eye make them suitable for most purposes: they are easy to work with.

Darners: Very long with long eyes. Their length enables many darning stitches to be picked up in one movement.

Bodkin: Long blunt-ended needles with a large eye, used for threading elastic through a casing or turning a rouleau.

Needles

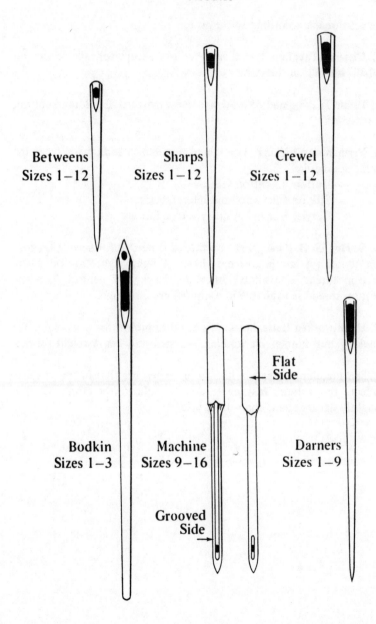

Betweens
Sizes 1–12

Sharps
Sizes 1–12

Crewel
Sizes 1–12

Bodkin
Sizes 1–3

Machine
Sizes 9–16

Flat
Side

Grooved
Side

Darners
Sizes 1–9

Dressmaking Simplified

Sewing Threads

Select threads according to purpose.

1. General Tacking: Use tacking cotton except for silk fabrics on which use silk or Terylene.

2. Tailor Tacking and Alterations: Use a mercerized coloured cotton, e.g. Sylko.

3. Permanent Stitching: Use where possible threads made from the same source, i.e.
>Cotton on cotton fabrics:
>Silk on silk, wool and linen fabrics:
>Terylene or nylon on synthetic fabrics.

4. Sewing on Buttons: A strong thread is needed for sewing buttons on to all top clothes except those of lightweight fabrics. Linen button thread is available in white, black and neutral. Terylene button thread is available in a limited colour range.

5. Hand-worked Buttonholes: A silk buttonhole twist is available for making buttonholes on woollen, worsted and heavyweight fabrics.

When matching threads with fabric, remember that lustre or sheen affects the colour, making it appear lighter; therefore, select a slightly darker shade than the fabric.

Threads

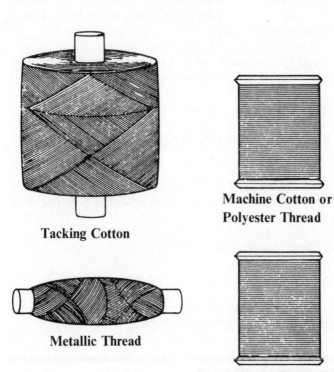

Tacking Cotton

Machine Cotton or Polyester Thread

Metallic Thread

Buttonhole or Saddle Stitching

Machine Embroidery Cotton

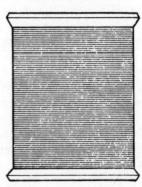

Large Reel of Machine Cotton

Dressmaking Simplified

Pressing Equipment

Iron: Thermostatically controlled to ensure safe heat for different fabrics. A steam iron is generally useful and it can be used as an ordinary iron, without steam.

Ironing Board: This should be covered with a detachable white cotton cover which is laundered regularly.

Sleeve Board: Also with a detachable cover.

Roller: Made from soft blanket, firmly covered with cotton fabric; used for pressing seams.

Pad: Made from layers of soft blanket encased with cotton fabric; used for pressing sleeve heads and parts that cannot be laid on to the board.

Damping Cloths: Made of soft, absorbent cotton fabrics.

Pin Board: For pressing velvets and corduroys.

It is essential that all pressing equipment is kept completely clean and damping cloths rinsed through after use.

Brief Guide to the Pressing of Fabrics

Cotton: Hot iron with a damp cloth or steam.

Linen: As these fabrics do not shrink, fullness cannot be eased away with pressing.

Silk: Moderate iron on the W.S. Do not use damp cloths as these, and sometimes the use of steam irons, may leave water marks.

Wool: Moderately hot iron and damp cloth are essential; fullness can be eased away by shrinkage. Always press wool fabrics under a cloth as wool scorches easily.

Rayon and Synthetic Fabrics: Generally a cool iron, without steam.

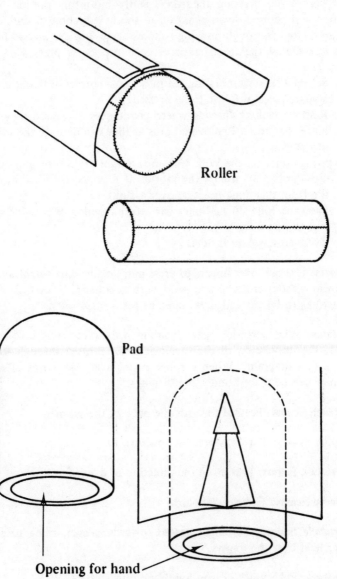

Pressing Equipment

Roller

Pad

Opening for hand

Dressmaking Simplified

General Rules

Pressing must not be confused with ironing which is a laundering process. When pressing, the iron is gently, but firmly, pressed down, lifted and pressed down again on to the next section of the fabric. Careful and thorough pressing is necessary to achieve a good finish. It is essential that each stage of each process is pressed as it is finished.

1. Set the thermostat dial on the iron to the correct heat and test on a spare piece of fabric to be pressed.
2. Remove tacking threads where possible as if pressed they may mark the fabric. Remove all pins as they can damage the surface of the iron.
3. Press fabric on the W.S. with the straight grain (pressing on the cross grain can stretch the fabric). If it is necessary to press on the R.S., this must be done over a cloth.
4. Press machine stitched lines flat before opening or pressing turnings to one side.
5. Do not press over fastenings.

Darts: Use pad over fingers to press point of the dart smoothly into fabric without creasing and press dart to either C.F. or C.B. if the dart has to be cut and press open as for a plain seam.

Seams: When pressing seam turnings open place over a roller so that the impression of the turnings is *not* pressed through to the R.S. (see diagram). When a roller is not available, strips of clean paper can be placed under the turnings.

French Seams: Pressed towards the back of the garment.

Waist Seams: Turnings pressed upwards.

Overlaid Seams: Pressed in the direction of overlay.

Sleeve Seams: Use sleeve board.

Armhole Seams: Turnings pressed towards sleeves, using pressing pad held over the fingers.

Gathers: Push point of iron lightly up into gathers.

Pleats: See section on pleats (page 76).

Sewing Machine

This is the most expensive piece of equipment that a needlewoman has to buy.

It is advisable to seek a personal demonstration of as many sewing machines as possible before making the purchase. This being impossible, she should consult a consumer group or magazine to find the best machine available in her price range. There are many different types and makes available so make sure that the sewing machine purchased can be serviced easily and that spare parts are readily obtained.

Sewing machines can be divided into four main groups

1. Straight Stitch: Hand, Treadle, Electric

Still manufactured in small numbers. Stitching is limited to forward and reverse straight stitching of various lengths. Presser feet are available for specific processes – gathering, binding, zip fasteners, (illustrated on page 22). It is important to know the make and model number of the sewing machine, as the foot which fits one model will not necessarily fit another.

2. Zig-Zag: Electric

Basic swing-needle machine. In addition to straight stitching, the needle swings from left to right to produce a zig-zag of varying length and width.

Works overcasting buttonholes, and by closing the stitch length, satin stitch for applique work.

3. Semi Automatic: Electric

In addition to zig-zag, four or five stitches are built into the machine.

(a) Three Step Zig-Zag or Serpentine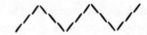

Used for overcasting on sheer fabrics to stop fabric from rolling over, woollen fabrics to prevent fraying and sewing on elastic.

(*b*) *Blind Stitch*

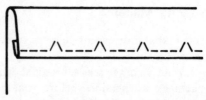

Usually four straight stitches and one zig-zag. Used for either invisible hems or for shell edging on fine fabrics.

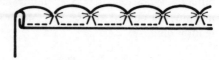

(*c*) *Elastic Blind Stitch*

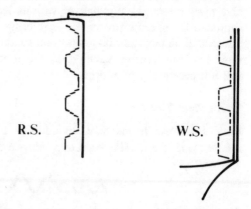

2/3 small zig-zags and one larger one.

Used for invisible hems on knitted or stretch fabrics or for decoration.

(*d*) *Multistretch Stitch*

R.S.   W.S.

Used for seaming together very elastic fabrics such as Helanca Lycra or towelling jersey.

4. Automatics and Superautomatics: Electric, Electronic

These sewing machines have the basic stitches with the addition of embroidery patterns. The patterns are produced by changing the programme on a dial selector or inserting cams or discs into the machine. A machine which has cams or discs can always be 'updated' by purchasing a new cam or disc as the pattern is released onto the market.

Superautomatics, in addition to having a left to right movement of the needle, have movement of the fabric forwards and backwards by the feed teeth.

(*a*) *Triple Straight Stitch*

This can stretch up to 75% again its original length, as it stitches two stitches forward and one back. Used on knitted fabrics for ordinary plain seams or on normal fabrics where the seam is under constant stress, e.g. armholes, sports clothes and trousers.

(*b*) *Overlock*

This produces a straight stitch seam and overlocks the raw edge in one operation. Stretches up to 100% its original length. Can be used to replace a french seam.

(*c*) *Super Stretch*

This is a triple stretch stitch and overcasting in one operation.

Recent developments have been made, whereby the speed of the motor can be controlled not only by the pressure on the foot control but also by a slide lever on the machine enabling the machine to stitch fast or very slowly without putting stress on the motor. The sewing machine often has electronic incorporated in its name.

General Care

1. Always keep the machine free from dust.
2. Keep the moving parts oiled but remove the surplus oil before using.
3. On an electric sewing machine make sure that the plug and flexes are in good condition, with no bare wires showing.
4. Check for loose screws.
5. Use the correct type of needle for the sewing machine.

Presser Feet that may be with the Machine

1.   Roll Hemmer   2.   Gather   3.   Hemmer

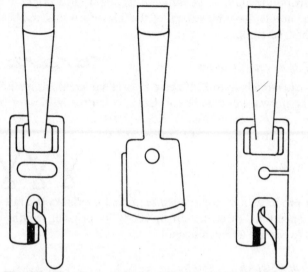

The handbook supplied with the machine will give instructions for attaching and method of use.

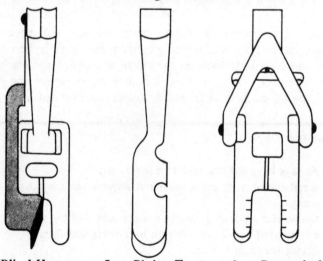

4.   Blind Hemmer   5.   Piping Foot   6.   Buttonhole

6. To prevent strain on the needle always pull the fabric towards the back of the sewing machine after use.
7. Never work a threaded sewing machine unless there is fabric under the pressure foot, as the thread quickly jams under the plate.
8. Never turn the wheel backwards.

Machine Stitching

Follow the instruction given in the handbook for the correct threading and manipulation of the machine. Test the stitching on a spare piece of double fabric on which you are working, unless you are doing gathers which should be tested on a single thickness of the material. Check that the tension is correct with a suitable length of stitch and size of needle.

Thick and Heavy Fabrics: 10 stitches to 2·5 cm   16 needle

Mediumweight Fabrics: 12 stitches to 2·5 cm   14 needle

Thin Lightweight Fabrics: 14 stitches to 2·5 cm   11 needle

Very fine slippery fabrics such as organza and chiffon: it is advisable to use a slightly loose tension and large stitch but with a *fine* needle. These fabrics pass through the machine more easily if the seam line is tacked through on to tissue paper which is torn away after machining.

Correct tension

Correct Tension: The stitch should appear the same from both sides and the thread be neither loose nor tight.

Top tension too loose

Incorrect Tension: When the top tension appears slack and the under thread has been pulled tight, tighten the tension screw slightly and test again.

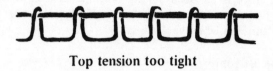

Top tension too tight

Common Faults and Possible Cause

In each case check the tension first and adjust if necessary.

Persistent Incorrect Tension: Incorrect threading of the machine or position of the spool.

Missed Stitches: Blunt or incorrectly placed needle.

Thread Breaking: Needle too fine or too coarse, or wrongly inserted: rough needle of poor quality: poor quality uneven thread.

Puckered Fabric: Blunt or too large a needle: fabric being *pulled* through the feed.

Broken Needle: fabric pulled towards the front of machine: pins or tacking knots on stitch line: too many thicknesses of fabric.

2 FABRIC FIBRES AND THEIR SOURCE

Until the early years of the 20th century fabrics could only be produced from natural fibres. With the rapid increase in the knowledge of chemistry and the extensive research of the scientists, man-made fibres have come into being—first, the rayon groups which are chemically processed from a vegetable base, and later, the pure synthetic fibres of a chemical source. All the man-made fibres are processed from a liquid. These new fibres are being constantly improved and varied in their processing to produce not only new fabrics with particular characteristics but fabrics that simulate the appearance and quality of fabrics of a natural fibre; and also yarn and fibres that may be mixed or blended to reduce any disadvantage of natural fibres. Basic fibres are of two main groups: *natural* and *man-made*.

Natural Fibres

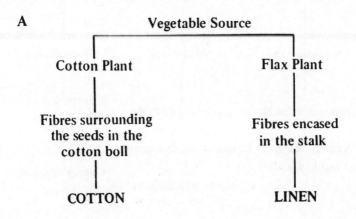

A   **Vegetable Source**

Cotton Plant	Flax Plant
Fibres surrounding the seeds in the cotton boll	Fibres encased in the stalk
COTTON	LINEN

Dressmaking Simplified

B

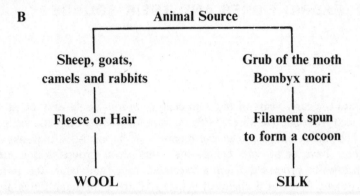

Animal Source

Sheep, goats, camels and rabbits	Grub of the moth Bombyx mori
Fleece or Hair	Filament spun to form a cocoon
WOOL	SILK

Man-made Fibres

C. Rayon

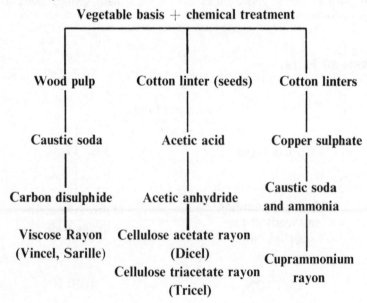

Vegetable basis + chemical treatment

Wood pulp	Cotton linter (seeds)	Cotton linters
Caustic soda	Acetic acid	Copper sulphate
Carbon disulphide	Acetic anhydride	Caustic soda and ammonia
Viscose Rayon (Vincel, Sarille)	Cellulose acetate rayon (Dicel) Cellulose triacetate rayon (Tricel)	Cuprammonium rayon

D.   Synthetic

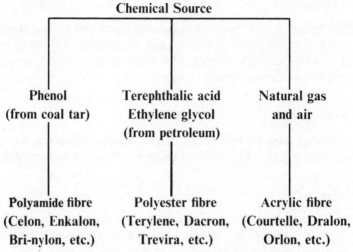

Chemical Source

Phenol (from coal tar)	Terephthalic acid Ethylene glycol (from petroleum)	Natural gas and air
Polyamide fibre (Celon, Enkalon, Bri-nylon, etc.)	**Polyester fibre (Terylene, Dacron, Trevira, etc.)**	**Acrylic fibre (Courtelle, Dralon, Orlon, etc.)**

Vegetable Fibres

Cotton

Source: the fibres that surround the seeds of the cotton plant: these are gathered after the cotton boll or seed pod has burst. The length and fineness of the fibres vary according to the area in which the cotton is grown.

Main region of growth: India, Africa and China. Egypt and West Indies (Sea Island cotton) produce the finest and longest fibres whereas the United States and Russia produce a shorter tougher fibre.

Production and processing: Great Britain imports large quantities of the raw material for the production of a wide range of cotton fabrics.

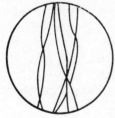

Cotton fibres under the microscope are seen to be flat with occasional twists.

Dressmaking Simplified

The spinning mills open and clean the baled cotton: the fibres are combed so that they lie parallel and are then drawn out in stages until a thin thread is formed. This thread is then twisted or spun to make a continuous thread or yarn.

WEAVING

The spun thread is transferred to the weaving mills where the yarns are coated with a starch-like substance to help the weaving process.

FINISHING

The woven cloth is inspected for faults and then sent to be bleached, dyed or printed to give the final appearance. Chemical finishes such as flame-proofing are carried out at this stage.

ADVANTAGES

1. Hardwearing even when the fabric is fine.
2. Launders well and is strong when wet: it can therefore be boiled or scrubbed if necessary.
3. Cotton is cool to the wearer; it is a good conductor of heat, taking warmth from the body and so is particularly suitable for summer or sports wear.
4. Absorbs moisture readily and it is therefore good for underwear and children's wear.
5. It takes dyes well and chemical finishes are taken easily.

DISADVANTAGES

1. Cloth tends to crease as cotton fibres have very little natural resilience.
2. Cotton is inflammable and flares up quickly.
3. Loosely woven cloth may shrink when washed.
4. Cotton fibres are weakened by strong sunlight.
5. Mildew may develop if stored damp or in a damp atmosphere.

Linen

Source: the long fibres that form the interior of the stem of the flax plant.

Main region of growth: Belgium, Northern Ireland and the Baltic States.

Production and processing: The flax plants are pulled up by the roots *without* breaking the stems and are sent to the mills where the seeds and leaves are removed. The fibres of the stem are encased in a woody casing containing gum: to remove the fibres the whole stems are placed in specially constructed ponds and soaked until the long strands are released and separated. The fibres are dried and then taken to the spinning mill where they are combed, spun and made into cloth in a similar manner to the cotton yarns.

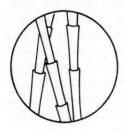

Linen fibres under a microscope are seen to be smooth, rounded and lustrous but notched at intervals.

ADVANTAGES: similar to those of cotton.

1. Hard wearing even when the fabric is fine.
2. Launders well and is stronger wet than when dry; even after repeated washing the surface remains smooth with no fluff: can be boiled if necessary.
3. Cool to wear as it is a good conductor of heat.
4. It absorbs moisture readily and, like cotton, is particularly good for use in hot climates.
5. The naturally smooth surface of linen makes it dirt resistant.

DISADVANTAGES

1. Linen tends to crease as there is little natural resilience.
2. It is inflammable.

3. Linen cloth is inclined to fray.
4. Mildew can develop if stored damp.
5. Is expensive as it is no longer grown in vast quantities.

Animal Fibres

Silk

Source: the cocoon of the silk moth (*Bombyx mori*).

Main regions of growth and production: Japan, China, India and Italy.

Production and processing: After hatching from the egg the silkworm lives for four to five weeks on mulberry leaves. When ready to spin into a cocoon it attaches itself to a twig and starts to spin the two filaments that are exuded from two tiny openings under the head: these continuous filaments are covered with a gum-like substance called sericu. Unless the cocoon is to be kept to hatch for breeding purposes, the chrysalis is killed by heat before it emerges as a moth so that the cocoon remains undamaged. The cocoons are then placed into tanks of warm water to soften the gum and then lightly brushed to find the ends of the continuous filaments; several ends are taken together through a guide lightly spun and wound on to a reel; the diluted gum then hardens again around the thread.

Silk fibres under a microscope show their smoothness and lustre.

Most silk fabrics are woven with the gum still on the threads; this is later removed by boiling the woven fabric. The broken filaments of cocoons that have been damaged by the moth emerging can be similarly removed, the short lengths being spun together and used for specific fabrics.

ADVANTAGES

1. Silk is a strong fabric even though it is fine.
2. Threads have a natural smoothness and lustre.
3. It is warm to wear as it is a *non*-conductor of heat.
4. It absorbs moisture readily and is comfortable to wear.
5. The natural resilience and elasticity of the filaments enables silk fabric to drape well and to be crease resistant.
6. It is non-inflammable.
7. Is moth proof.

DISADVANTAGES

1. Most silk fabrics, apart from the fine washing silks, are difficult to launder.
2. Stains and watermarks easily.
3. It is expensive.

Wool

Source: The fleece or hair of sheep and goats, also of camels, rabbits, llama and vicuna goat. The length and quality of the fibres varies according to the breed which is usually associated with a particular geographical area.

Main regions producing raw wool in quantity: Australia, New Zealand, South Africa and Argentina.

Production and processing: Great Britain imports quantities of wool to supplement her own supplies in order to produce a wide variety of woollen fabrics. In the manufacture of raw wool into yarn there are two distinct processes, one for worsted yarn, and a second for woollen yarn or cloth. Worsted yarn is prepared from the long strong fibres

Wool fibres under a microscope are seen to be constructed of overlapping scales.

only, all the weak short fibres being removed by combing. The long fibres are straightened, laid parallel and spun in a similar manner to cotton fabrics to produce a smooth regular yarn which is then woven into *worsted* cloth. *Woollen* yarn is prepared from all the short or broken fibres kept from the combing of the worsted yarn. When spun, the many ends stick out from the yarn, giving it a rough bulky appearance: similarly, all short-fibred fleece and hair is spun for woollen fabrics.

With either type of woollen fibre, the percentage of sheep's or other wool should be specified on all wool fabrics claiming to include or be made of wool other than sheep's wool.

MAIN VARIETIES

Cashmere: made from the wool of the Kashmir goat.

Mohair: from the coat of the angora goat, a native animal of Turkey.

ADVANTAGES

1. Wool is warm to wear and is a non-conductor of heat: the individual fibres trap the air which acts as an insulation helping to retain the body heat.
2. It absorbs moisture readily and is comfortable to wear.
3. Natural resilience and elasticity make the fabric crease-resistant and adaptable to handle in the making of tailored garments as fine woollen fabrics drape well.
4. As wool contains natural oils it is water-repellent.
5. It is non-flammable but inclines to smoulder.

DISADVANTAGES

1. Weak when wet, the fibres soften and the fabric will stretch easily.
2. Wool requires careful laundering: it must not be washed in hot water; rubbing, scrubbing or wringing tightly causes the fabric to felt as the scales on the individual fibres become interlocked. Often better to have dry cleaned.
3. Is prone to damage by moth.

Man-made Fibres

Rayon

Made from vegetable sources of cellulose treated with chemicals to produce a liquid from which filaments can be manufactured and processed into cloth.

VISCOSE RAYON

Source: wood pulp reduced to a thick glutinous liquid by the action of caustic soda and carbon disulphide.

Production of the filament: the liquid is forced through the tiny holes of a spinneret to eject long continuous filaments which congeal on contact with the air; they are further hardened by treatment with sulphuric acid. The fineness of the filaments is determined by the size of the holes in the spinneret.

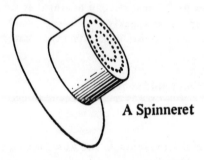

A Spinneret

ACETATE RAYON AND TRIACETATE RAYON

Source: from cotton linters treated with acetic acid and acetic anhydride, the resulting liquid being dried into flakes.

Production of the filament: The flakes are dissolved in acetone and the sticky liquid produced is forced through a spinneret and ejected into a current of warm air to solidify the filaments.

CUPRAMMONIUM RAYON

Source: from cotton linters treated with copper sulphate, caustic soda and ammonia.

Production of the filament: the liquid is forced through a spinneret and the filaments hardened in a chemical tank; they also become more elastic and can be drawn out to finer degrees of thinness.

Manufacture of cloth: rayon yarns can be processed to produce a wide variety of fabrics, i.e.
(a) *Filament yarn:* the continuous filaments are spun together and woven to produce smooth fabrics such as satin and taffeta.
(b) *Staple yarn:* the filaments are cut into shorter lengths and spun to produce a more bulky yarn for heavier weight fabrics.

ADVANTAGES

1. Resemblance to silk fabrics but less expensive.
2. A poor conductor of heat but not as warm as wool.
3. Is absorbent and dries quickly.
4. Generally crease-resistant: triacetate rayon can be permanently pleated.
5. Drapes well.
6. Is moth proof and mildew resistant.

DISADVANTAGES

1. Requires careful laundering as the fibres are easily damaged by rough or heavy handling.
2. Is easily damaged by chemicals such as acids and bleaching agents.
3. Can be damaged by excessive heat, dry or moist.
4. Inflammable, some rayons flaming quickly.

Polyamides (Nylon)

Source: Air (oxygen and nitrogen), water and coal (phenol).

Production of the filament: the basic substances are blended, melted down and processed to form polymer chips. The chips are then melted and the liquid forced through a spinneret to form filaments which solidify on contact with the air; these filaments are smooth and rod-shaped.

Ban-lon   **Taslan**   **Crimp forms**

Production of the cloth: the basic filament can be processed before weaving to produce a variety of fibres. Textured nylons include:

BAN-LON: the filaments are set in a zig-zag formation: when spun together they produce a soft bulky yarn with a degree of elasticity.

TASLAN: the filaments are passed through a jet of air which creates loops on the individual filaments. These produce a yarn which is soft but does not stretch.

CRIMP FORMS: these are soft and stretchy yarns produced mainly by twisting processes which are usually doubled with yarns twisted in the opposite direction.

The woven fabrics can also be processed, e.g. permanently pleated, or brushed which gives a soft bulky finish to the R.S. of the fabric.

ADVANTAGES

1. Is very strong: although light in weight it is so strong that nylon ropes are often used for shipping and in industry.
2. The basic filament is elastic and resilient: it can be stretched considerably and still return to its original length.
3. The smooth surface of the filament repels loose dirt to a certain degree and is easy to launder.
4. It dries quickly at room temperature and needs little or no pressing.
5. It is crease-resistant but can be heat set for permanent pleating.
6. Is moth proof.
7. Is inflammable.

DISADVANTAGES

1. Frays easily.
2. Can be damaged by some acids and bleaching agents but is not harmed by alkaline cleaning fluids.
3. Is non-absorbent and is not suitable for young children's wear or for sportswear for use in summer.

Polyester

Source: ethylene glycol and terephthalic acid (both from petroleum).

Production of filament yarns: the basic substances are processed to produce an ivory coloured plastic which when solidified is cut up into chips: these polymer chips are melted at a high temperature and forced through a spinneret. The polyester yarn is then produced in two distinct forms:

(a) *Filament fibre:* as the filaments are ejected from the spinneret, and solidify, they are wound on to cylinders as 'undrawn' yarn; this yarn is then drawn and stretched to several times its original length and then wound on to bobbins.
(b) *Staple fibre:* as the filaments come from the spinneret they are brought together into a thick bundle called a 'tow' and then drawn out. The 'tow' is then artificially waved and set by heat, chopped into specific lengths and then spun in the usual manner.

ADVANTAGES

1. A strong fibre but with slightly less strength when wet.
2. It is easy to launder and dries quickly; it requires little ironing.
3. Is crease-resistant but can be heat set for permanent pleating.
4. Is smooth, soft and drapes well.
5. It is not damaged by dry cleaning agents, alkaline or acid substances when used in moderation.
6. It has a high resistance to damage by light and sunlight through glass and is therefore ideal for curtains.
7. Is both moth proof and resistant to mildew.

DISADVANTAGES

1. Polyester fibres are not absorbent unless mixed with other fibres.
2. The fabric frays easily.

Acrylic Fibres

ORLON: manufactured by Du Pont.

ACRILAN: manufactured by Chemistrand.

COURTELLE: manufactured by Courtaulds.

Source and production: these fibres are formed from a compound called Acrylonitrile which is made from natural gas and air. The filaments are made with the use of a spinneret and are then processed in the same way as the polyester *staple* fibre.

ADVANTAGES

1. Strong.
2. It is warm to wear as the air is trapped in the staple fibre.
3. Is easy to launder and dries quickly.

Blends and Mixtures

Blended fibres: yarn that is spun from two or more different fibres.
  At first, only man-made fibres in staple form were used but now scientists have produced new filament yarns.

Bicomponent yarns: two filaments of different chemical composition are fused together during the spinning process to form a double filament. These yarns can be textured by subjecting them to heat or moisture. The two chemicals react differently, one shrinking or swelling against the other.

Filament blended yarns: these are produced by a combination of two different filaments twisted together to form a yarn. The best known example is Tricelon, a blend of Tricel (a brand of triacetate rayon) and Celon (a brand of nylon), which gives the strength of nylon to the lustrous, but not so strong, rayon fibres.

Mixtures: fabrics which are woven from two or more different yarns, e.g. polyester warp with woollen weft.

Fibres are mixed or blended to obtain the advantage of each fibre and to counteract the disadvantages, e.g. polyester and linen. Linen has the main disadvantage in that it creases badly; polyester is crease-resistant: therefore, by mixing, the fabric is less crease-resistant than polyester but is more resistant than linen. The mixing or blending of fibres can reduce the cost of the fabric, e.g. silk mixed with a fine woollen yarn: as the fibres are similar in construction the characteristics are little changed but the cost is lower than if the fabric were of 100 per cent silk. The properties of mixed or blended fibres depend on the proportion of the fibres used: the fabric should be treated in the same way as fabrics made from the fibre of the highest proportion.

It is important to choose the correct fabric for your garment. Choosing a fabric which is unsuitable for its purpose will mean that the garment will never be the success it could have been. When you use a commercial pattern you will notice, on the back of the envelope, a list of suggested fabrics for the garment you have chosen. This is a useful guide especially where the use of knitted fabrics is being considered.

The important points to take into consideration when choosing a fabric apart from the colour and pattern are:

1. *Weight.* Choose a fabric suitable for the time of year and for the purpose of the garment.
2. *Laundering.* Remember that clothes in regular use should be made of a fabric which can easily be laundered.
3. *Content of fibre.* Find out the percentage of the main fibres to obtain the properties of the fabric.
4. *Texture.* Choose soft plain fabrics, perhaps with a slight sheen, for intricate draped styles but use more highly textured bulky fabrics for outdoor wear.

See page 239 for a 'Table of Suggested Fabrics for Everyday Garments.'

3 PERSONAL APPEARANCE

To be well groomed and dressed in a becoming manner gives confidence to the wearer.

Good grooming requires careful thought and choice in the selection of colour, style and fabric in order that they may enhance the good features whilst dispensing, or at least minimizing, those which are less attractive. It is not necessary to follow fashion slavishly but important to pick out the trends and details that are adaptable to your own style and personality.

General Rules for Good Grooming

1. Wash hair, face and body regularly.
2. Keep nails clean and well manicured and teeth well cared for.
3. Keep make-up fresh and carefully applied.
4. Use a deodorant and if necessary an anti-perspirant daily.
5. Press heavily creased garments after use.
6. Brush outer garments before replacing them in a wardrobe and allow garments to air overnight before storing.
7. Regularly wash and dry clean garments.
8. It is important to make sure that all buttons are firmly sewn on.
9. Hems should be level and securely fastened in position.
10. Make sure that no seams are coming apart and all repairs are carried out as soon as is necessary.
11. Petticoats and linings should not show beneath the hem line of the garment.
12. Shoulder straps should be kept firmly in place under the dress or blouse. Make a shoulder strap guide in sleeveless dresses or these may be purchased in a haberdashery department.
13. Always wear white underwear with white or pale coloured garments.
14. Stockings and tights should be free of holes or ladders and washed daily.
15. Shoes and handbags should be cleaned regularly as well as when necessary.

Dressmaking Simplified

Budgeting

When it has been decided how much money can be spent on clothes each year, it is best to plan the major items first. However, the full scope of the budget must be kept in mind, which will include the whole wardrobe and its maintenance.

Allowance must be made for all accessories, dry cleaning and shoe repairs in addition to top clothes which will include casual and sportswear, summer and winter wear. Also the requisite underwear for the top clothes, nightwear, socks, stockings, tights and footwear.

Remember that the British climate can seldom be trusted to provide long spells of warm weather so allocate money for summer dresses accordingly and *do not* be tempted in the spring to buy several of the new season's lightweight dresses, which at the end of a poor summer may be scarcely worn and be out-dated by the next summer season.

Coats and suits are the main items in the budget, choose a style that is not of high fashion so that it will not be out of date by the next year. It is wise to buy the best that you can afford as a good coat or suit should last at least two seasons and poor quality clothes soon appear shabby and become out of shape. When planning new purchases remember the clothes that you have so that the new clothes can integrate with them in use and therefore widen the possibilities of different combinations.

Ready-made clothes—whenever possible, try on the garment to make sure that it both suits you and fits well, thereby you may avoid an expensive mistake.

Store sales—by buying carefully you may be able to extend your budget, look for well known trade names of fabrics and clothes which have been genuinely reduced. Beware of cheap quality goods that may have been 'bought in' for the sales.

Avoid buying goods in a hurry without proper consideration, take time to select and if undecided leave the problem and return when a proper decision has been made.

Colour

The choice of colour is most important as it should enhance the looks of the wearer, her personality and the style of the garment.

Study the colour of your eyes, hair and complexion, always try to compliment the eyes which are the focal point of your expression.

Those with fair colouring can wear most colours well, in particular the softer shades. Vivid colours can best be worn by those with dark hair or sallow skins so these provide a definite contrast. People with high complexions, red or auburn hair often look best in cool colours such as green or blue.

Dark colours have a slimming effect whereas pale colours which have more impact, have an enlarging effect.

Be adventurous whichever colour is in fashion, one of its shades will suit you even if only a small proportion is worn such as a scarf. Ensure however that it will combine with your existing clothes—often unusual but interesting and satisfactory combinations can be achieved this way.

Style and Choice

The type of figure that you have, its proportions and characteristics should be considered when selecting the style of a garment. Determine which are the good and bad points of your figure and look for a style which will disguise the bad ones.

To disguise the faults naturally gives emphasis to the better points of a figure. It is foolish to choose a style which you will find very attractive but does not suit you.

It is necessary to consider the purpose of the garment and the practicality of the style. It is also important to consider the colour and texture of the fabric to be used.

Dressmaking Simplified

Tall and Angular Figure

Choose: 1. Separates of contrasting colour.
2. Double-breasted coats and jackets.
3. Fabric with bright bold patterns.
4. Dresses that fall from the shoulder or yoke lines.
5. Well tailored trousers.

Avoid: 1. Tight fitting garments.
2. Clinging fabrics.
3. Outfits in one colour.

Short and Slim Figure

Choose: 1. Clothes with style lines taking the attention from the waist line.
2. Skirts pleated into waist.
3. Soft colour and one colour outfits.
4. Small printed patterns.

Avoid: 1. Bulky fabrics.
2. Large prints.
3. Large tight belts.
4. Part-coloured outfits.

Tall and Angular

Correct

Incorrect

Short
and Slim

Correct

Incorrect

43

Dressmaking Simplified

Tall Plump Figure

Choose: 1. Simple styles without fussy frills.
2. Interesting collar and neck line.
3. Separates that by-pass the waist lines.
4. Matt surfaced fabrics.

Avoid: 1. Clothes that have intricate style lines.
2. Sleeves with pleats or gathers at sleeve head.
3. Fabrics that cling or have shiny surfaces.
4. Bold all-over pattern.
5. Pale colours.

Short Plump Figure

Choose: 1. Simple styles with vertical tucks or seams.
2. Straight dresses, perhaps with a narrow centre panel.
3. 'V' neck lines.
4. Fabrics with vertical stripes or small all-over patterns.

Avoid: 1. Anything tight or waisted.
2. Frills.
3. Separates that contrast too much in colour.
4. Fabrics which are either bulky or with large bright patterns.
5. Trousers.

Tall and Plump

Incorrect

Correct

Short and
Plump

Correct

Incorrect

Dressmaking Simplified

Figure with a Large Bust

Choose: 1. 'V' neck lines.
2. One-piece dress or with hip line interest.
3. Separates with a dark top and light skirt.

Avoid: 1. High neck lines.
2. Empire line dress.
3. Frills on the bodice.
4. Tight belts and tightly fitting waist.
5. Short sleeves.

Figure with Large Hips

Choose: 1. Styles that hang from the shoulder or a chest yoke line.
2. Interesting neck line detail.
3. Separates with a bright top and dark-coloured skirt.

Avoid: 1. Trousers.
2. Hipster skirts.
3. Shirt or full-bottomed sleeves.
4. Tight belts at waist or hip level.

Large Bust

Correct

Incorrect

Large Hips

Correct

Incorrect

47

4 TAKING MEASUREMENTS

It is necessary to be accurate when taking measurements, check that the tape measure is correctly placed.

All round measurements require added allowance for ease of movement—as given below.

Before taking the measurements determine the waist position by tying a piece of tape firmly but comfortably around the waist.

Do NOT pull the tape measure too tightly.

Position for taking measurements: as illustrated opposite

1. Bust   + 5 cm ease   taken around fullest part
2. Waist + 2·5 cm ease
3. Hips   + 5 cm ease   taken around widest part
4. Chest width
5. Back width
6. Shoulder
7. Length of Back   C.B., neck bone to waist
8. Length of Skirt   C.B., waist to hem
9. Length of Arm   shoulder point, round elbow to wrist bone
10. Wrist   + 2·5 cm ease
11. Top Arm + 2·5 cm ease

When buying a paper pattern it is necessary to know your bust, waist, and hip measurement and the length required. If these come between stock sizes select the larger size and alter where necessary—see page 50. The measurements listed above are needed when checking a paper pattern or for drafting a personal pattern. As good paper patterns are available in so many styles, time may be wasted by attempting to draft a pattern for a style similar to one that can be bought already drafted and marked.

Positions for Measuring

Front   Back

5 PATTERN ALTERATION

It is often necessary to make small adjustments to a bought paper pattern in order that the main measurements may correspond with your personal proportions (see previous page).

In order to retain the balance of the garment alterations should be made as required, at the positions indicated in the diagrams.

Basic methods of general alteration only are given, final points of alteration should be assessed and made when the garment is fitted. NOTE: Remember that paper patterns *include* allowance for ease and for turnings.

To Reduce the Measurements of a Pattern

At the appropriate position crease the paper and make a pleat equal in width to half the amount to be reduced, pin into position. For alterations in width, the excess amount should be divided between the back and front and equally between left and right sides of the garment.

To correct the seam lines it may be necessary to add a strip of paper and to re-draw the line as illustrated in Diagram 3.

Diagrams 1 and 2 illustrate:

(a) Pleats pinned in back and front bodice to reduce width at shoulder, bust and waistline.
(b) Position line to reduce length from neck to waistline between bust and waistline.
(c) Method to reduce the armhole by pinning a piece of paper behind the pattern and drawing in a new line to raise the under-arm.

Diagram 3

(a) Width of sleeve reduced from shoulder to wrist.
(b) Length of sleeve reduced between shoulder and elbow and elbow and wrist.
(c) Correction of seam line.

Pattern Reducing

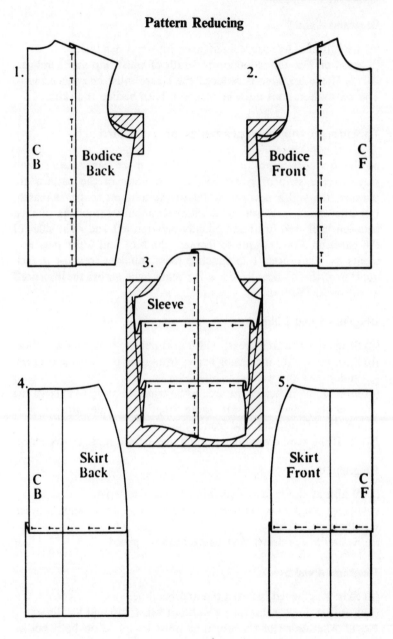

Diagrams 4 and 5

(a) Length of skirt reduced—between hips and hemline.
(b) Position line for reduction in width of waist, hip and hemline.
NOTE: If the armhole is reduced the sleeve must be reduced also. The waist alterations must be made on both bodice and skirt.

To Enlarge the Measurements of a Pattern

At the appropriate position line cut through the paper pattern and place over a strip of paper so that the edges of the pattern are parallel, the width between equal to the amount to be increased. For alterations in width the additional amount should be divided between back and front and equally between left and right sides of the garment. For example to increase the bust and waist measurements by 5 cm insert 1·25 cm strip from shoulder to waist in each quarter of the bodice. Re-draw the seam lines across the insertions as shown in Diagram 3.

Diagrams 1 and 2 illustrate:

(a) Strips inserted to increase width at shoulder, bust, and waistline.
(b) Position line for increasing length from neck to waistline between under bust and waist.
(c) Dotted line indicates the area to be trimmed away to enlarge the armhole, check that the same length of under-arm seam is removed from back and front bodice.
NOTE: If the armhole is enlarged the sleeve head must be deepened.

Diagram 3:

(a) Width of sleeve increased from shoulder to wrist.
(b) Sleeve lengthened between shoulder and elbow and between elbow and wrist.
(c) Seam lines re-drawn and sleeve head deepened.

Diagrams 4 and 5:

(a) Skirt lengthened between hip and hemline.
(b) Position line for increasing width of waist, hip and hemline.
NOTE: Alterations of the waistline must be made on both bodice and skirt.

Pattern Enlarging

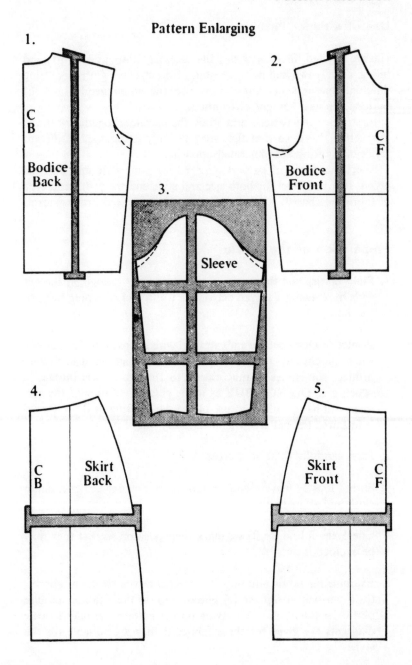

1. Bodice Back — C B

2. Bodice Front — C F

3. Sleeve

4. Skirt Back — C B

5. Skirt Front — C F

Dressmaking Simplified

Use of a Paper Pattern

Having selected the pattern buy the necessary amount of fabric and lining, usually two and more versions of the style are given, requiring different amounts of fabric. Buy also the recommended size of buttons, zip and amount of trimmings.

First, open the pattern and study the markings together with the instruction sheets so that they may be fully understood. Different styles of marking are illustrated opposite.

Select the pieces of pattern required for your style and find the layout that is correct for both size and style and the width and type of fabric purchased. Replace the pieces not required in the packet.

Preparation of the Fabric

1. **Plain fabrics and those with a woven pattern**—straighten the cut ends by drawing a thread across the width and trimming back to this line.

   Printed fabrics—cut the ends straight with the pattern. Be cautious when purchasing printed fabrics as they can be inaccurately printed, sometimes as much as 15 to 16·5 cm off the thread, in which case DO NOT BUY as if the pattern is followed the garment will hang badly because of the bias cutting or if the thread is followed the pattern will be seriously out of place.

2. Press carefully if fabric is creased.

3. Shrink loosely woven woollen fabrics by pressing under a damp cloth and allowing to dry in the air.

4. Check the fabric for flaws, mark their position so that they may be avoided if possible.

5. Examine the fabric and note if it has (a) woven stripes or checks, (b) a one-way design or (c) pile or nap, as these fabrics require particular attention when laying on the pattern. Usually specific diagrams are given for these fabrics if they are suitable for the style.

A Guide to Commercial Pattern Markings

MEANING	PERFORATED	PRINTED
Lay to the Fold		
Straight of Grain		
Fitting Line or Seam Allowance		
Notches or Balance Marks		
Darts		
Centre or Fold Lines		
Pleats		
Button and Buttonhole Positions		

Dressmaking Simplified

General Layout of a Pattern

1. Follow the correct layout diagram, fold the fabric as directed and spread squarely and smoothly on the cutting out table.
2. Lay out all the pattern pieces required to ensure that there is sufficient fabric.
3. Check the position of each piece, so that the necessary pieces are placed to the fold and that the straight threads (or print) are parallel with the markings for the straight thread.
4. Pin the pattern in place with the pins near the seam allowance and at right angles to the edges.

The fabric must be kept flat on the table and each piece smoothed out as it is pinned.

NOTE:
1. When using fabric with a one way pattern or pile follow the instructions given on opposite page.
2. When using printed fabrics with a definite motif and woven patterned fabrics follow also the instructions given for checks and striped fabrics on page 58.

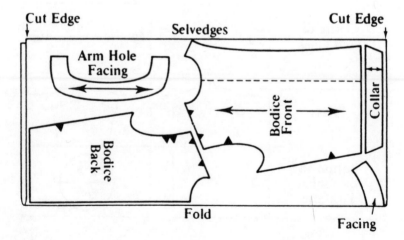

One-way Fabrics

Extra yardage is usually necessary when using fabrics with:

(a) one-way print
(b) one-way arrangement of woven stripes.
(c) **with nap**—woollen and mixture fabrics with surface fibres lying in one direction only. These should be cut so that the fibres run down towards the hem.
(d) **with a cut pile**—silk velvets with the pile lying upwards and velveteens, needlecords and corduroy with the pile running downwards—made up in this way the fabric has a richer colour.

It is essential that all pattern pieces are laid in the same direction, main sections can rarely be interlocked for economy of fabric.

Fabric may be folded in half lengthwise but *must not* be folded across the width as this will reverse the pattern on pile.

When laying out on woven stripes, one-way prints and prints with a definite repeat motif also follow the instructions for check and striped fabric given overleaf.

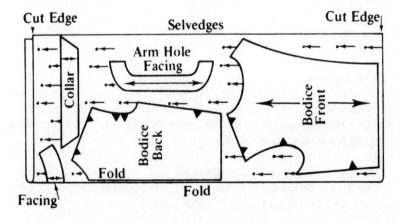

Dressmaking Simplified

Checks and Striped Fabrics

To gain a professional finish it is essential that the checks and stripes match in line at the shoulder, under-arm and side seams, C.B. and C.F. lines, hemline and all seams of the skirt. Therefore extra fabric must be allowed.

1. Ensure that fabric is folded correctly so that all lines are exactly in position one over the other, see diagram.
2. Place the pieces to be laid against the fold first and position the other pieces accordingly.
3. Place the balance marks, centre and hem lines of the sections to be joined in identical position on the checks or stripes, see diagram below.

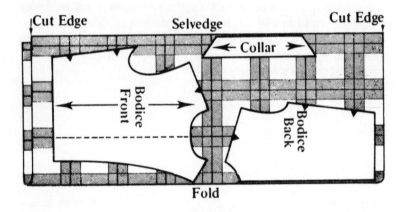

Cutting Out

1. Check that all the required pieces have been pinned into position and there is enough space for pieces that have to be duplicated and for crossway stripes if necessary.

2. Cut with long even strokes along the edge of a perforated pattern or along the thick black line of a printed pattern. DO NOT lift the fabric up from the table whilst cutting.

3. Cut the balance marks (notches) outwards from the pattern. DO NOT cut into the seam allowance, this causes general weakness and prevents possible alteration.

4. When cutting out the lining use the correct line marked by folding away the surplus area of the paper pattern.

Marking out the Pattern

Tailor tacking, page 65, Diagram 1, is the best method of transferring the pattern markings on to the double fabric as both layers can be accurately marked together. Use one coloured thread for balance marks, another for darts and fitting points, another for the position of buttonholes and so on. Mark all centre lines and pleats with straight tacking, page 66. Mark with straight tacking the fitting line through single fabric of all curved and detailed sections and small pieces following the fitting lines across seam allowance.

For speed, if the fabric has been *accurately* cut, long smooth lines may be left and later tacked together with the use of a marker made to correspond with the width of the seam allowance.

N.B. Use a fine silk thread for marking all silk and very fine fabrics.

Alternative methods

Tailors' Chalk—this can be used if the garment is to be tacked together and made up directly after cutting out, as it will brush off with handling. It cannot however mark both layers at the same time so these must be parted and marked separately, therefore ensure that sleeves are paired and right and left sides marked correctly. DO NOT use on a fabric with a satin weave.

Carbon paper—this may be used with care on washable fabrics only, otherwise possible alterations may be visible. Place the carbon paper between the fabric and the pattern with carbon (shiny) side against the fabric, transfer the markings with a pencil. Double layers have to be marked separately as with tailors' chalk.

Dressmaking Simplified

Preparation for Fitting

After transferring the pattern markings, remove the main pieces of paper pattern and separate the double or folded pieces, cutting through the tailors' tacks, page 65, Diagram 2. Run in gathering threads where necessary, see page 67, prepare tucked areas of fabric, see page 84, put in gathering threads for any smocking.

Tack together the main sections of the garment in the following order:—

1. Darts and pleats.
2. Panel lines, shoulder and under-arm seams of the bodice (not the collar or facings).
3. All sections of the skirt.
4. Tack the skirt to the bodice and ensure that the position of the opening is correct.
5. Tack together a sleeve but do not insert.

When preparing a skirt for fitting the best results are obtained if the waistband is fully made up, with the interfacing and tacking it into place on the skirt. This enables the position and measurement of the waistline to be checked thoroughly.

When tacking darts and seams first match and pin together all balance marks and fitting lines carefully. Accuracy at this stage is most important. Place the pins at right angles to the fitting line.

Fitting

1.

Looseness across the
shoulders lifted up into
the shoulder seam

2.

Neck Line fullness
taken into darts

3.

Weft

Warp

Sleeve hanging
correctly

Sleeve set in with
too much fullness
at the front

4.

Folds showing that
the waist is too tight

5.

Folds showing skirt
too tight on the hip-line

Fitting the Garment

Try the garment on R.S. out and study the following points:—

Mark any necessary alteration on the right-hand side only and transfer these to the left-hand side after the garment has been taken off.

1. Note the hang of the garment both back and front, check that the centre lines are perpendicular.

2. With a garment that has a waistline check that this corresponds with the natural waistline of the wearer. Raise or lower if necessary but first assess the shoulder line.

3. Note the shoulder fit, if there is looseness across the back, snip the tacking and raise the back bodice and re-pin the shoulder seam. Diagram 1. For sloping shoulders the seam will need to be taken up at the shoulder point.

4. The back neck edge, if this is too loose or wide the extra fabric should be taken in to form a small dart each side of the C.B. Diagram 2.

5. Check the position, length and fit of the bust darts, especially the side bust dart which may be too long or wrongly placed. After the shape, length and, if necessary, the position to suit your personal figure, but allow ease for movement.

6. Width of garment, it there are any visible lines across the garment these denote tightness. Diagrams 4 and 5. Release the tackings at the side seams and re-pin to give a looser fit with a *smooth* seam line. Similarly, if width is too loose re-pin side seams to give tighter fit.

7. Correct waist darts if necessary but ensure that all darts correspond on skirt and bodice.

8. Pin the sleeve into the armhole to achieve the correct hang, and position ot ease to give a smooth finish without tight wrinkles or fullness.

9. Assess neckline, position of fastenings and any trimmings.

To Transfer the Alterations

Remove the garment carefully. Replace the pins marking the alterations with a new tackline on each section. Separate the pieces and accurately fold the right-hand side over the left and pin through the new tackline to the left side. Following the line of pins tack in the new fitting lines.

NOTE: When fitting and marking alterations the pins are placed along the fitting line.

6 CONSTRUCTION OF A GARMENT

Order of Work

1. Preparation of fabric and cutting out.
2. Mark the pattern on to the fabric.
3. Run the gathering threads and tack pleats in position.
4. Tack together basic sections of garment for fitting.
5. Fitting and alterations if necessary.
6. Separate sections and transfer alterations to left-hand side of garment. If major alterations, refit and separate again.
7. Disposal of fullness—darts, pleats, tucks or smocking.
8. Shoulder seams and panel lines.
9. Make and attach pockets, prepare bound buttonholes.
10. Collar.
11. Front and neck facings, completion of bound buttonholes.
12. Worked buttonhole.
13. Side seams and skirt seams.
14. Wrist opening, sleeve seam, cuff and/or sleeve edge neatening.
15. Insert sleeve, face armhole if no sleeves.
16. Join skirt to the bodice.
17. Plackets and zip fasteners.
18. Hemline after final fitting.
19. Final press.
20. Attach buttons, hooks, eyes, and press studs.

NOTE: Press *each* stage as it is completed.

Temporary Stitches

These are needed for marking out pattern lines or holding two or
more layers of fabric in position, ready for permanent stitching.
All tacking stitches are removed after final stitching.

Tailor Tacks

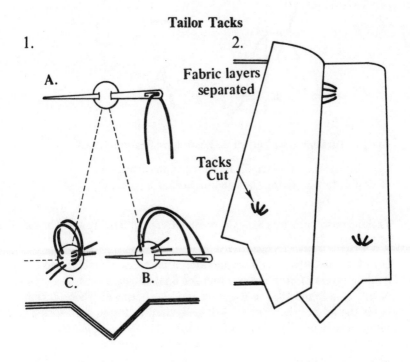

1.

2.

A.

Fabric layers
separated

Tacks
Cut

C. B.

Tailor Tacking

Use: for marking through *double* fabric, the position of darts,
buttonholes and other parts of construction.

Using a double thread, work double stitches, leaving long loops
(shown in Diagram 1), then gently pull the two layers apart and cut
through the stitches, leaving half of the thread in each layer of fabric.

Upright Tacking or Basting

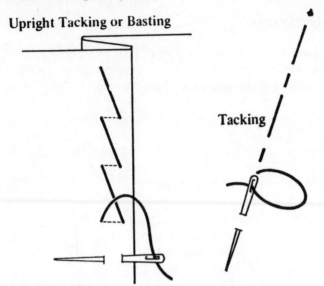

Tacking

Upright Tacking (also known as Basting or Diagonal Basting)

Use: for holding in place pleats, revers, interfacings and other areas of double fabric during the construction of a garment.

Tacking (also known as Straight or Flat Tacking, Basting and Thread Marking)

Use: for marking fitting lines and alteration on *single* fabric and for holding layers of fabric in position for final stitching.

NOTE: It is found that to use long and short stitches when tacking holds the fabric more firmly. A knot is used to fasten on a tacking thread and a double stitch to fasten off.

Permanent Stitches

These are stitches essential in the construction of a garment, each with a particular purpose for which it should be used.

The quality of the completed garment depends on the high standard of *hand finishing*. However, for speed, certain of these processes can be worked by machine with the use of the appropriate attachments.

Machine Stitching (plain)

Used in general for speed to replace hand back stitching: see page 19 for details of the sewing machine and its use.

Hand Stitching

All hand sewing should be neat and firm with even stitches. The size of the stitch has to be adapted to the thickness of the fabric. Before starting, experiment with a few stitches to find the most suitable size for the fabric.

Fasten on thread with 2 or 3 small back stitches on sewing line. Fasten off with 2 or 3 small stitches worked into the back of the completed stitching.

1. **Running Stitch   Right to Left**

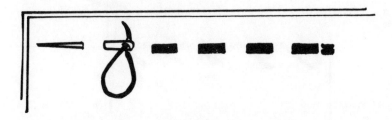

Use: gathering, tucking, hand-sewing of fine fabric.
Stitches and spaces between should be of equal length.

2. **Back Stitch   Right to Left**

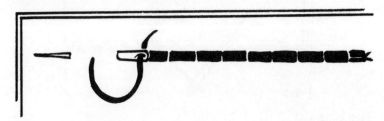

Use: hand-sewn details and decoration, tucks and seams.
Stitches should be equal in length with no space between.

3. Oversewing   Right to Left

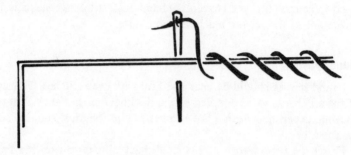

Use: for joining two folded or selvedge edges, neatening of double raw edges, details of construction and strengthening, joining and application of lace.

4. Overcasting   Left to Right

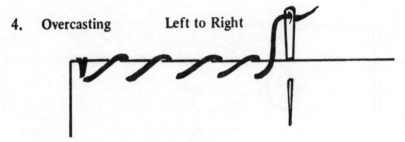

Use: neatening raw edge of *single* fabric.
NOTE: Work from *left* to *right*.

WS   R to L

Hemming

Use: holding folded edges firmly in place. Slope and space of stitch are equal and appear the same on both sides.
NOTE: *Not* used for dress or skirt hems.

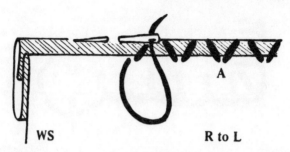

WS   R to L

Slip Hemming

Use: holding skirt, dress and other folded edges in place. Invisible on R.S.

NOTE: Do not pull up thread tightly. Pick a single thread of fabric only at A. For alternative method see page 203.

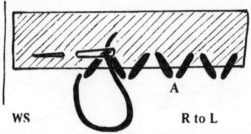

WS   R to L

Catch Stitch

Use: holding single edges such as interfacings. Invisible on R.S.

NOTE: When working on single fabric, pick up single thread of fabric only at A.

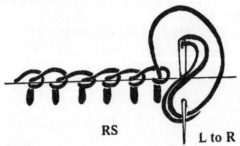

RS   L to R

Buttonhole Stitch

Use: buttonholes (see details on page 144). Work so that the knots rest on top of the raw edges. Stitches should be one thread apart.

NOTE: Upright position of needle.

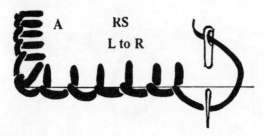

Loop Stitch

Use: neatening raw edges with stitches touching (as at A) for strengthening weak points. Decoration.

NOTE: Correct spacing of stitches to form a square. Placing of stitches at corner.

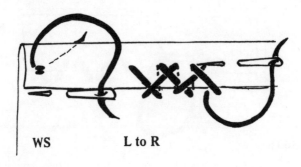

Herringbone Stitch

Use: holding hem of thick fabric. Flannel patch. Work across a single raw edge. Decoration.

NOTE: Placing of the needle position (see diagram).

7 DISPOSAL OF FULLNESS

Fullness of material is an important feature of the style as well as a necessity for ease of movement in a well-fitted garment. Whereas fashions change the following basic methods of controlling fullness frequently recur, though adapted to enhance the current style.

Darts

These are a stitched fold of material which is tapered to a narrow point. They are used to make a garment fit smoothly; to give room for movement where necessary and to dispose of fullness where desired, for example at the waistline. Darts are often arranged to form part of the style lines of the garment.

Single Pointed Dart

1. Fold fabric R.S. together matching fitting line carefully. Pin and tack. Diagram 2.
2. Starting from the wide end, machine stitch on fitting line until the fold is reached, then continue for three more stitches along the fold. Diagram 3.

   (This with careful pressing, will ensure a smooth finish on R.S.)
3. Remove tacks and press stitching.
4. Press waist darts towards the C.F. or C.B. line. Press under-arm darts towards waistline, shoulder darts towards the neck and elbow darts towards the wrist.

NOTE: If the finished dart is more than 2 cm wide at the base the fold should slit as far as the dart is 1·25 cm wide, the turnings then pressed open, trimmed and neatened as shown in Diagram 4.

Single Pointed Dart

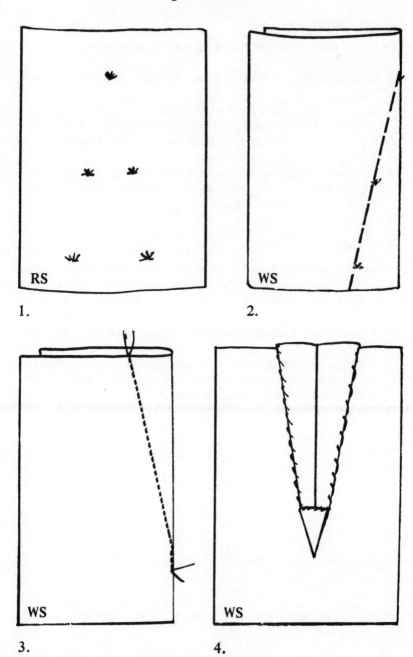

1.

RS

2.

WS

3.

WS

4.

WS

Double Pointed Dart

These are used on dresses and coats which have *no* waists.

1. Fold fabric R.S. together, matching fitting line carefully. Pin and tack.
2. Machine stitch along the fold three stitches below lower point of dart. Follow the fitting line out to the waistline and up to the top point and along fold for three more stitches. Diagram 2.
3. Remove tacks and press stitching.
4. To prevent dragging on the R.S., the dart turning must be snipped at the waistline to 0·3 cm of the stitching. Neaten the raw edges with loop stitch. Diagram 2.

Dart Tuck

These are open-ended darts similar to tucks. Apart from styling they are often used for waist darts on blouses and shoulder darts on coat and jacket linings.

1. Fold fabric R.S. together, matching fitting line carefully. Pin and tack.
2. Starting from the wide end, machine stitch on the fitting line to end of dart tuck, reverse machine stitching for 1·25 cm to finish and strengthen the stitching. Diagram 4.
3. Remove tacks, press stitching and press to correct position.

Double Pointed Dart

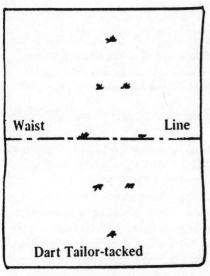

Waist — — Line

Dart Tailor-tacked

1.

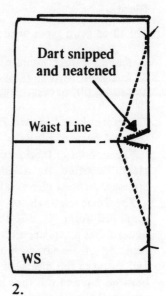

Dart snipped and neatened

Waist Line

WS

2.

Dart Tuck

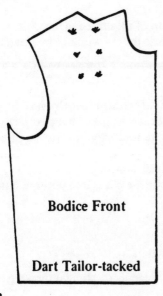

Bodice Front

Dart Tailor-tacked

3.

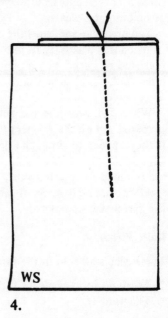

WS

4.

Pleats

The three main types of pleating are:

1. Knife Pleating: equal with pleats folded in the same direction.
2. Box Pleat: two knife pleats folded over away from each other.
3. Inverted Pleat: two knife pleats folded towards each other.

Therefore these last two kinds used continuously form alternately box and inverted pleats.

The amount of fabric required is three times the finished width of pleat. Therefore, for a knife pleated skirt three times the finished hip measurement plus turnings must be allowed for.

The basic methods of preparing these pleats are shown in a simplified form. It will be found when following a commercial pattern that pleats are either (a) slightly flared 1·25 cm wider at the hem and a little narrower at the waist which gives an excellent hang and swing to the pleats, or (b) that they are overlapped or widened between hip and waistline in order to decrease the hip measurement to that of the waist.

For all pressed and stitched pleats, the edge of the fold should be thread-marked and accurately pressed back from waist to hem *before* assembling the pleats.

The arrow → indicates the direction of fold to be made.

When it is necessary to join the fabric for the width to be pleated, it should be joined with a plain seam that is arranged to come at the inner fold of a pleat so that it is invisible with as little extra thickness as possible.

When the waistline (or setting-in of pleated panels) has been prepared, try on the garment to check that the pleats hang correctly; if they appear to drag, the deep inside fold may have to be lifted slightly to correct this *before* the final stitching. Firm waist finishes are required for pleated skirts of heavier fabrics.

After pleating has been finished, baste the pleats into position until the garment is completed.

Knife Pleats

These pleats all fold in the same direction.

1. Mark position of pleats, tack lines, keeping on straight thread (see Diagram 1).

A–A' = twice the depth of the pleat.

A'–B = depth of pleat between fold edges on R.S. (see Diagram 2).

2. Fold and press accurately each pleat edge A, B and C.
3. Fold edge A to line A'. Pin and diagonal baste securely into position.
4. Fold edge B to line B', pin, baste and continue.
5. Machine stitch to the required length along folded edge. Fasten off securely. See Diagram 2.

1.

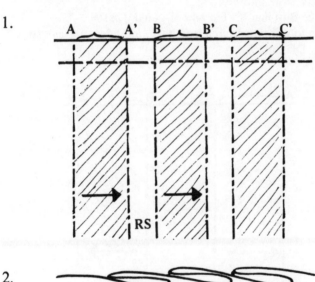

2.

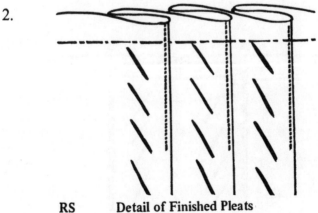

RS   **Detail of Finished Pleats**

Box Pleats

These are made by two knife pleats folded away from each other (which forms an inverted pleat on W.S.).

1. Mark position of pleats: Diagram 1.
   A–A' = twice depth of pleat.
   A'–B = twice depth of pleat = width of box pleat on R.S.
   B–B' = twice depth of pleat.
2. Fold and press accurately each pleat edge A' to line A. Pin and diagonally baste into position.
3. Fold edge B to line B': Pin and diagonally baste.
4. Stitch on fold from required length to waist edge. Fasten ends off securely. Diagram 2.

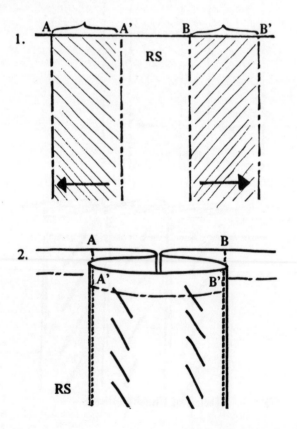

Alternative Method with no Visible Stitching
1. With R.S. facing, pin and tack together lines A–A'.
2. With R.S. facing, pin and tack together lines B–B'.
3. Stitch lines to required length. Remove tacks.
4. With care diagonally baste inside pleats into position.

Inverted Pleats

These are made by two knife pleats folded towards each other (which forms a box pleat on the W.S.).

1. Mark position of pleats: Diagram 1.
    A–B = twice depth of pleat.
    B–A' = twice depth of pleat.
    A'–C = twice depth of pleat = distance between inverted pleats on R.S.
2. Fold and press accurately each pleat edge A, A', C, C'.
3. Fold edge A to line B. Pin and diagonally baste into position.
4. From top of pleat stitch folded edge to length required, turn fabric under machine and stitch upwards on second folded edge. See Diagram 2.

Alternative Method with no Visible Stitching
1. With R.S. facing, pin and tack together lines A–A'.
2. Stitch to required length. Remove tacks.
3. Open pleat equally so that line B is in position behind stitches line. Press and diagonally baste carefully into place.

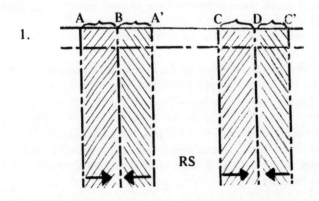

1.

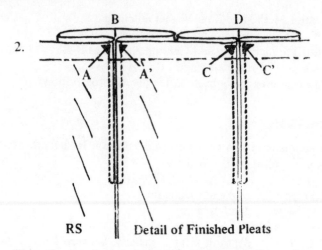

Note the two inverted pleats have formed a box pleat

Kick Pleats

This pleat, which has no stitching visible on R.S., allows for movement in a straight skirt and is inserted at the base of centre back seam, side or panel seams. Patterns usually allow additional seam allowance for this pleat. If the fabric pulls easily and the pleat is liable to strain, an arrowhead should be worked in for reinforcement of seam ending.

1. Complete the machine stitching for the plain seam as far as the pattern mark. Do not remove the tacking which holds the unstitched section in place.
2. Place the underlay of the pleat into position. Pin and tack on to the seam allowance.
3. Machine stitch underlay to each side of seam allowance and across the top of the pleat (see stitching on diagram opposite).
4. Neaten the raw edge at top of underlay with herringbone.
5. Neaten the raw edges by the same method and as a continuation of the seam neatening. When edge stitch neatening has been used generally in the garment, neaten raw edges of pleat with oversewing. Remove tacks and press. If necessary, complete with an arrowhead on R.S.

Kick Pleat

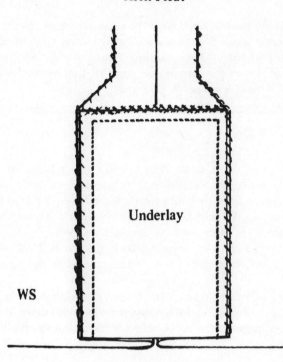

Underlay

WS

Arrowhead

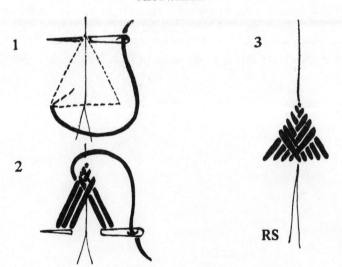

1

2

3

RS

Dressmaking Simplified

Arrowheads are used to strengthen the seam ending at the top of a kick or inverted pleat. It is placed so that the lower straight edge is level with top of pleat. Use buttonhole twist for stitching. Method of work is shown in the diagram on page 81, first by marking the outline of the triangle shape.

Tucks

A decorative method of controlling fullness by a number of small pleats evenly spaced and stitched to the required depth. On children's wear they can be used to hold extra fabric allowed for growth, in particular around the skirt hem. Completely tucked fabric (with no released fullness) is often used for decorative panels.

Width of tucks can vary from pin tucks 0·15 to 1·25 cm and are machine stitched, hand run or sewn with decorative stitch (see overleaf).

Allowance of extra fabric is twice finished width of each tuck. Measure, stitch and press into position each tuck before starting the next. Complete all the tucks before marking out the pattern or fitting lines.

Markers

For ease in measuring, prepare a cardboard marker with cut notches to show required width between folded edge of completed tuck and edge of the next tuck.

For wide tucks also indicate width of tuck, see diagram opposite.

1.   Wide Tucks

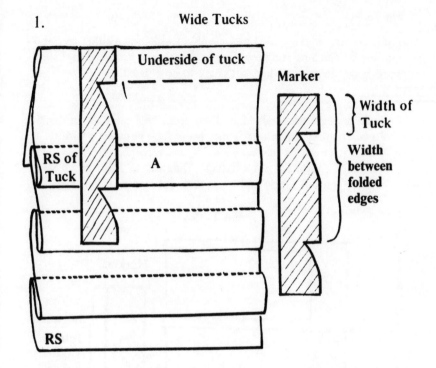

Wide Tucks

Prepare marker as required. Start work from the side to which tucks are to be pressed.

1. Fold the fabric along the thread R.S. out for the edge of the first tuck. Tack width of tuck.
   Stitch from top on R.S. of tuck. Remove tacks and press stitching.
   Open out fabric and press tuck flat into position.
2. With fold towards marker, as at point A, place marker correctly and fold back fabric for edge of second tuck and tack width of tuck. Diagram 1.
   Stitch from top side of tuck, remove tacks and press.
   Open out fabric and press tuck flat into position.
   Repeat.

Pin Tucks

These are tiny edge stitched tucks 0·15 cm wide, sewn either by hand running or machine stitching. Prepare marker as required and start work from the side to which tucks are to be pressed.

1. Fold fabric along the thread R.S. out for the edge of first tuck. Tack if necessary and edge stitch from top on R.S. of tuck. Press stitching. Open out fabric, press tuck flat into position.
2. With fold towards marker as at A, place marker correctly and fold back fabric for second tuck. Diagram 2. Edge stitch and press. Open out fabric and press tuck flat into position. Repeat.

2. **Pin Tucks**

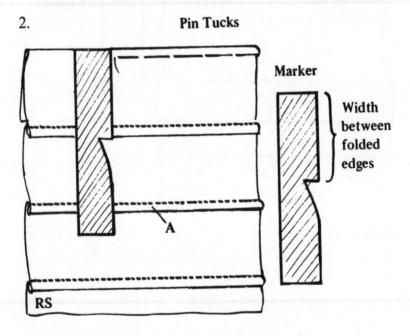

Marker

Width between folded edges

A

RS

Decorative Tucks

Shell Tucks

Suitable for blouses and children's wear of fine fabrics. Follow method given for wide tucks on page 83.

1. Prepare and tack width of tucks 0·6 cm or less.
2. Work shell edging from top on R.S. of tuck. Open out fabric and lightly press into position.
3. Prepare second tuck and repeat process.

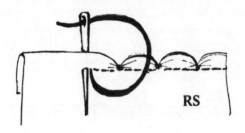

Hem-stitched Tucks

Suitable for lightweight fabrics of a loose weave which allows for threads to be withdrawn easily.

1. Mark edge with tack line.
2. Draw out a thread for finished width of tuck from each side of fold line. Draw further threads for width required towards the fold line, so that two lines of drawn threads are prepared.
3. Fold fabric on edge line with drawn threads exactly opposite. Tack into position. Work hemstitching from underside of tuck and press.
4. Open out fabric and press tuck flat into position, Measure distance for fold of second tuck as method given for wide tucks. Mark edge of fold with tack line and repeat process.

Wide tucks can also be stitched decoratively with stem, chain, whipped, running stitches or french knots.

Methods of tucking lightweight fabrics: suitable for large areas or whole garments such as over blouses and dresses: tack all fabrics before marking pattern, using machine stitching for speed.

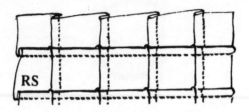

Cross Tucking: pin tucks. Tuck fabric in one direction first and then at right angles. Effective when styled to be cut on the cross.

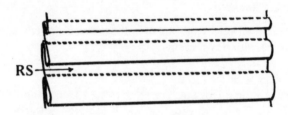

Graduated Tucking: wide tucks. Increase depth of tucks towards hem.

Gathering

Fullness of lightweight fabrics at waist, yoke and wrist can be controlled by gathering to give an even finish of fine unstitched tucks. Gathered sections are set in with either a plain seam or an overlaid seam which can have a decorative finish.

Small amounts of fullness, such as sleeve heads, can be eased away smoothly with the aid of a gathering thread (see page 183). Two rows of gathering should be worked, the first 0·3 cm below the fitting line and the second 0·3 cm above the fitting line. Do not attempt to gather more than one section or width of fabric with one thread. After the setting-in seam has been made, the gathering thread below fitting line *must* be removed.

Gathering by Hand

Fasten on the thread securely and work two rows of fine running stitches. The stitches of the second row must be placed directly in line with those of the first row. For ease in drawing up, work the second row in the opposite direction so that the thread can be drawn from each end.

Gathering by Machine

The longest stitch with a loose tension must be used. Place stitches of second row in line with those of the first. Draw up *one* of the machine threads only for each row, otherwise the fabric will not move.

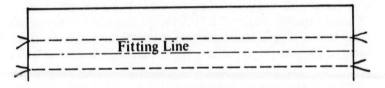

Drawing Up: Draw up both lines together, gently easing fabric along, until correct width is reached. Hold threads temporarily in place by twisting round vertical pin. Disperse gathers evenly.

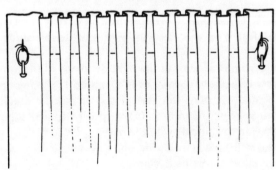

Smocking

This is a decorative method of controlling an area of fullness: as the method and tension of work is not rigid, it provides for elasticity and ease of movement.

The allowance of fabric required is usually four times the finished width of smocking. On very fine fabrics, a greater allowance may be needed and a small piece of fabric should be gathered and drawn up to check this. It is advisable to check all fabrics in this way as the amount required does vary according to the fabric and depth of pleat required. When drawn up the pleats should just touch but should *not* be tightly packed.

Preparation for Smocking

On check, striped or spotted fabrics, the pattern should be used as a guide for putting in the gathering thread.

On plain or freely patterned fabrics, a transfer of smocking dots can be used: these are available in yellow and blue and with different spacing according to depth of pleat required. The transfer should be cut to the correct length and depth of the section to be gathered.

Place the transfer on the W.S. with the spots in line with the thread of the fabric. With a moderate heat press the iron over the dots, peeling off the paper immediately after the iron has passed. On sheer fabric the transfer must be pinned into position and the gathering worked through the paper which is then torn away, as the transfer spots would be visible on the R.S. if ironed on.

The top line of gathering is placed 0·3 cm above fitting line. Gathering lines should be approximately 0·6 cm apart to hold the pleats firmly in position.

Use a sufficient length of strong cotton separately for each line of gathers and fasten on securely with a knot or double stitch.

1. Working from R.S., start at the right-hand end of the top line and work row of gathering *either* as in Diagram 1, picking up a small stitch behind each dot (for fine pleats) *or* passing needle in and out of dots as in Diagram 2. On striped or similar fabrics, plan the gathering to coincide with the pattern, i.e. to pick up the same coloured stripe. When drawn up, this would give a different coloured effect to the main fabric.

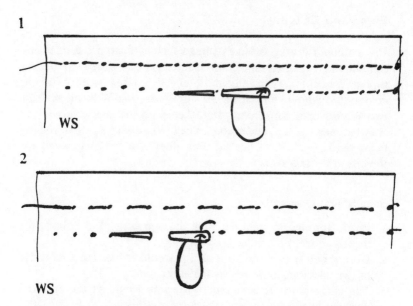

WS

2. When all rows have been stitched, draw up in pairs, starting at the top. Until drawing up is complete, twist the gathered threads round vertical pins (see page 89). When all rows have been drawn up evenly and the gathered area is the exact width required, tie off the loose ends (Diagram 3).

NOTE: Gathering threads must not be removed until the smocking has been completed.

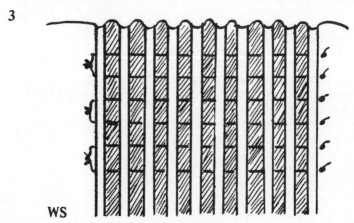

WS

Dressmaking Simplified

Smocking Stitches

Use a smooth firm embroidery thread such as Cotton à Broder or a suitable number of stranded cotton threads or a twisted embroidery thread. Smocking is usually most effective when worked in one colour throughout. Fasten on all stitches on the W.S. by working two stitches over the second pleat, then push the needle through to R.S. between the first and second pleat. Work with an even, slightly loose tension so that smocked area does not contract, when the threads are withdrawn.

Stem Stitch: Diagram 1

1. Work from left to right stitching through each pleat holding the thread above the needle.
2. Do not pull thread too tight as this would reduce the final width of the smocking and prevent the elasticity.
3. The chain stitch is achieved by turning round at the end and working back with the stitches close together.

Cable Stitch: Diagram 2

1. Work as for stem stitch but alternate the thread above and below the needle.
2. The double cable is worked by stitching another row under the first, with the lower stitch of the first row touching the upper stitch of the second row.

Wave Stitch: Diagram 3

Work as the diagram making sure that there is the same number of stitches (going down as coming up) on each side of the wave.

Working downwards the thread is *above* the needle and working upwards the thread is *beneath* needle.

Smocking Stitches

The stitches shown on this page are all worked from
LEFT TO RIGHT

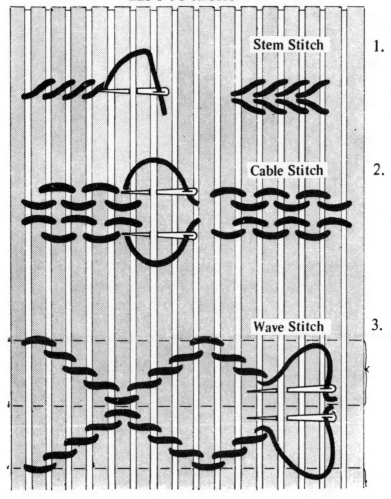

1. Stem Stitch

2. Cable Stitch

3. Wave Stitch

Smocking Stitches cont.

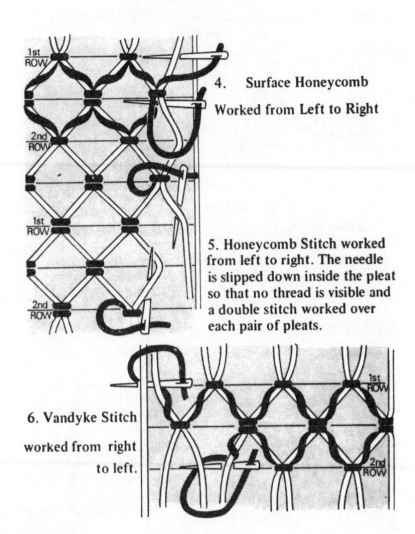

4. Surface Honeycomb
Worked from **Left to Right**

5. Honeycomb Stitch worked
from left to right. The needle
is slipped down inside the pleat
so that no thread is visible and
a double stitch worked over
each pair of pleats.

6. Vandyke Stitch
worked from right
to left.

Elastic Casing

This should be the width of the elastic plus 0·6 cm. It is necessary to
work a buttonhole slit in the W.S. of the casing for the insertion and
removal of the elastic.

Casing in the Hem

1. Turn hem on the marked line. Machine stitch into place.
2. Machine second line of stitching, width of casing from the first stitched line.
3. Cut a slit across the casing on the W.S. only of the hem and neaten with buttonhole stitch.

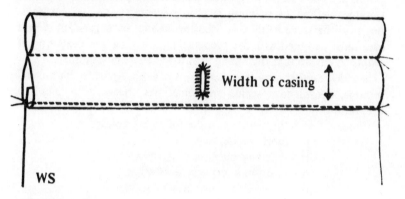

WS

Within a Facing

1. Cut facing width of casing plus turning.
2. Cut a slit, width of elastic plus 0·3 cm across the centre of facing and neaten with buttonhole stitch.
3. Tack the facing into position.
4. Machine stitch each edge. Remove tackings and press.

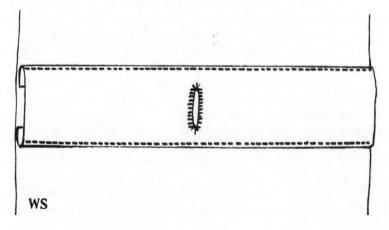

WS

8 SEAMS

Seams are essential for all garments and it is important that the most suitable method of seaming is chosen in each case: as far as is practical the same method is used throughout each garment. Great care must be taken with the preparation, stitching and neatening of seams to ensure that they hang well with clean smooth lines.

Seams are either *inconspicuous* or *conspicuous*. Apart from practical reasons, conspicuous seams are sometimes chosen as a detail of decoration.

Choice of seam depends upon the following points:

        (a) fabric being used.
        (b) type and purpose of garment.
        (c) position and purpose of seam.
        (d) the style line or curve of seam.

The methods most generally used and their purpose and advantages are given in the following pages.

General points to be followed when making all seams:

1. Match balance marks and fitting line (or amended fitting line) carefully and pin into position correctly, that is, with the pin entering the fabric on fitting line and coming out in seam turnings (see Diagram 1). *Do not* pin along or parallel with the fitting line.
2. Tack firmly along fitting line and remove pins. Both these stages are *essential* as two or more layers of fabric easily move out of position when stitched either by hand or by machine unless held firmly with a tacked line.
3. Stitch or machine stitch exactly against the fitting or tacked lines so that these are not caught into the permanent stitching and can be removed easily. Remove tacks.
4. Press each stitched line first and *then* press turnings open or to one side as necessary.
5. It is essential when seaming knitted or stretch fabrics that the machine stitching has elasticity. Therefore either use the special stretch stitches on the sewing machine or set the swing needle dial setting to a slight zig-zag and proceed as usual.

Plain Seam: inconspicuous

The flattest method of seaming and is used generally but in particular for non-fraying fabrics and *all* thick fabrics. This seam requires neatening to prevent the raw edges from fraying: the most suitable method should be chosen according to fabric and position of seam. See details on page 97.

1. Place R.S. together of pieces to be joined, matching balance marks and fitting lines carefully. Pin and tack in position (Diagram 1). Remove pins.
2. Stitch along fitting lines, remove tacks, and press stitching.

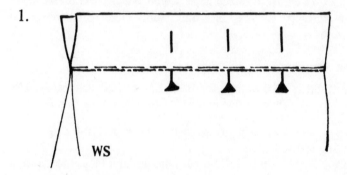

3. Pressing turnings open (Diagram 2) ready for neatening. See page 97.

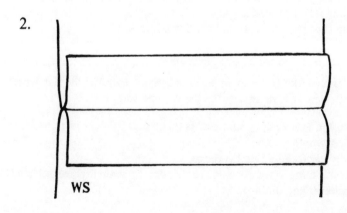

Methods of Neatening of Plain Seam

Flat Edge Neatening: Diagram 1.

1. Trim seam turnings equally 1·25 cm.
2. Neaten with either (a) hand overcasting, (b) machine stitched overcasting, (c) loop stitch.

Edge Stitching: Diagram 2

Suitable for firm fabrics only: is neat, hard wearing and launders well.

1. With R.S. of seam turning uppermost, fold the raw edge under to a line 1 cm from stitching line. Tack.
2. Stitch 0·15 cm from folded edge. Remove tacks and press.
3. Trim turnings on W.S. of seams evenly close to stitching: see point A.

Binding: Diagram 3

This method is used mainly for thick fabrics that fray easily. Use either thin silk fabric or fine nainsook binding, toning in colour.

1. Prepare crossway strip: see page 108 and page 110 for details of binding method.
2. Place R.S. of strip to R.S. of turning, pin and tack into position so that the stitch line is 0·6 cm from seam line. Stitch, remove tacks and press.
3. Trim raw edge to 0·5 cm. Press binding strip upwards.
4. Fold strip over raw edge to W.S., turn in raw edge of strip and place fold against stitch line.
5. Hem the fold on to stitch line. See point A.

Neatening of a Curved Seam: Diagram 4

In order that the turnings of a curved plain seam can be flat when pressed open, it is necessary for them to be snipped.

1. As often as necessary snip across turning to 0·3 cm of stitched line (Diagram 4).
2. Loop stitch the single raw edge.
3. Press turning open. Neaten remainder of seam by the selected method (Diagram 4b).

Seam

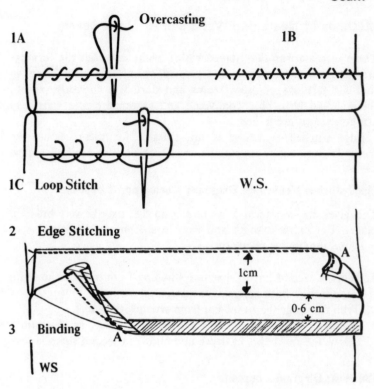

Overcasting

1A   1B

1C   Loop Stitch   W.S.

2   **Edge Stitching**

A

1cm

0·6 cm

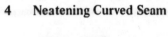

3   **Binding**

A

WS

4   **Neatening Curved Seam**

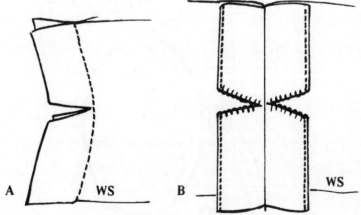

A   WS   B   WS

Methods of Neatening Waist and Armhole Seams

These seams are usually joined with a plain seam but the turnings are neatened together and not pressed open. Care must be taken that the turnings of other seams and darts are correctly placed: these should have been completed and neatened *before* waist and armhole seams are joined.

Edge stitched neatening is not suitable for these seams; the methods given below are suitable for either waist or armhole seams.

Hand-stitched Neatening: Diagrams 1 below and 2 opposite

This gives the smoothest finish to a seam that may be very bulky in places. For extra strength and ease in stitching, a further line of machine stitching is necessary.

1. Work a second line of machine stitching 1 cm outside the fitting line through both layers of turnings.
2. Trim raw edge 0·3 to 0·5 cm from second stitch line.
3. Overcast, as Diagram 2 opposite, or loop stitch, as Diagram 1 below, the raw edges to depth and taking in second stitched line.

Bindings: Diagram 2 opposite

See notes and instructions on page 110. On waist seams place stitch line of binding 1 to 1·25 cm from seam lines.

1.

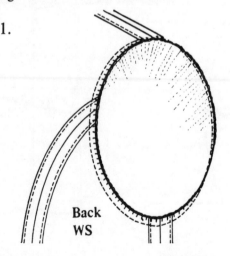

Back
WS

2.

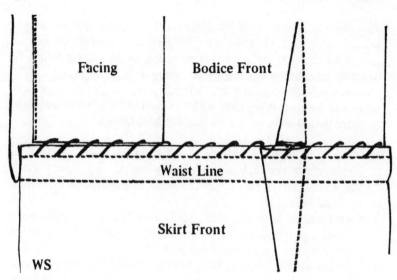

3.

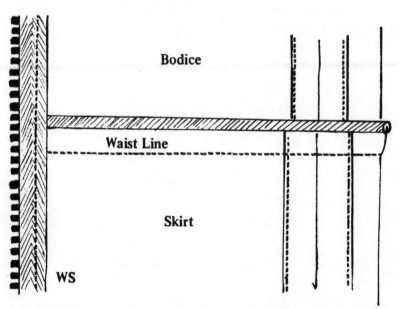

French Seam: inconspicuous

This seam is mainly used for lingerie, fine blouses and children's wear. If possible it should always be used on sheer fabrics such as chiffon when used singly, i.e. not mounted on to a lining fabric. It can only be used on fine fabrics as otherwise it is too bulky.

A french seam is strong and self-neatening as all raw edges are enclosed; therefore it launders well. Finished width of seam must not be more than 0·6 cm or less on fine or sheer fabrics.

1. Place W.S. together, matching balance marks and fitting lines carefully. Pin and tack through fitting line.
2. Machine stitch 0·6 cm outside the fitting line (Diagram 1); less on very fine fabrics.
3. Press turnings open and trim to 0·3 cm or less. Pressing the turnings open at this stage and before trimming, makes the following stages easier and produces a successful finish.
4. Turn the work through to W.S. Fold back on the stitched line and tack fitting lines together again. Stitch on fitting line, thereby enclosing raw edges (Diagram 2).
5. Remove all tacks, press stitching and then press seam over towards the back of the garment (Diagram 3).

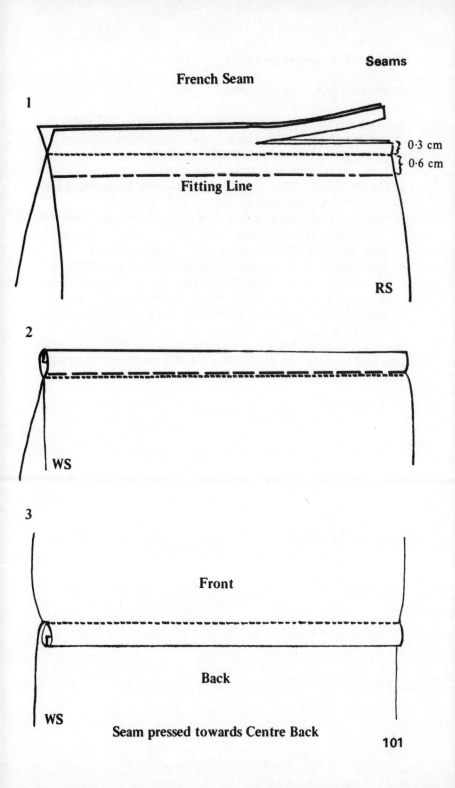

Seams

French Seam

1

0·3 cm
0·6 cm

Fitting Line

RS

2

WS

3

Front

Back

WS

Seam pressed towards Centre Back

Overlaid Seam: conspicuous

A strong seam used for joining difficult shaped pieces, e.g. yokes and shaped panel lines. As stitching is visible it emphasizes style lines and can therefore be planned as a decorative detail.

1. On the overlay, fold seam allowance to W.S. along fitting line. Pin and tack (Diagram 1).
2. Place the folded edge against fitting line of underlay, matching balance marks. Pin and tack.
3. Edge stitch the fold from R.S.; remove tacks and press.
4. Trim turnings level to 1 cm and neaten together with either loop stitch or oversewing (Diagram 2). When neatening, a second line of machine stitch may be worked as in the method of finishing waist and armhole seams as described on page 99.

On children's wear, blouses and lingerie, a decorative stitch is sometimes used instead of edge stitching. Suitable stitches would be stem, chain or interlaced stitch (see page 230).

Overlaid Seam

1.

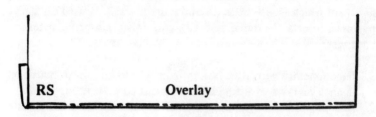

RS   Overlay

Fitting Line

Underlay

RS

2.

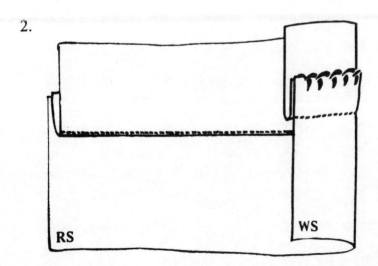

RS   WS

Dressmaking Simplified

Machine and Fell: conspicuous

This is known as run and fell if worked entirely by hand; it is a strong flat seam which is self-neatened and launders well. Is used on shirts, pyjamas, shorts, trousers, overalls and other garments receiving hard wear.

1. Place together with R.S. facing the pieces to be joined, matching balance marks and fitting lines. Pin and tack on fitting line.
2. Machine stitch along fitting line. If worked by hand use a close running stitch. Remove tacks and press.
3. Trim seam allowance of back or lower section of garment to 0·6 cm (a little less for finer fabrics). Trim second seam allowance evenly to 1·25 cm width (Diagram 1).
4. Fold projecting raw edges over lesser one with fold line even width 0·6 cm from stitching and tack (Diagram 2). Press folded edge.
5. Open out fabric so that joined pieces are flat and press folded edges into position: press iron away from stitch line. Pin and tack flat.
6. Hem neatly the folded edge: remove tacks and press (Diagram 3a). Hemming will be invisible on R.S. (Diagram 3b). For correct placing of intersecting seams see page 106.

Machine and Fell Seam

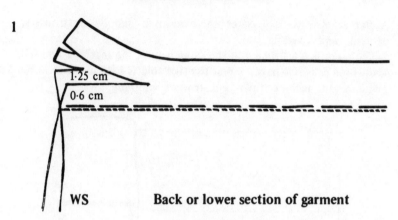

1

1·25 cm

0·6 cm

WS

Back or lower section of garment

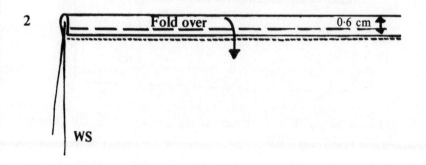

2

Fold over

0·6 cm

WS

3

RS

B

A

WS

Double Machine Stitched Seam: conspicuous

A flat seam with raw edges enclosed used mainly for trousers, pyjamas and overalls.

The seam is constructed in the same way as the machine and fell seam—see previous page, *except* that the fold is held in position by a line of top machine stitching instead of hemming.

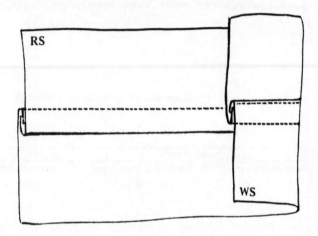

When joining different sections of the garment note the correct direction of the overlap.

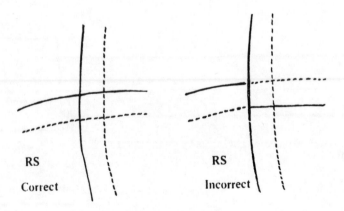

9 CROSSWAY STRIPS

These are narrow strips of fabric cut at an angle of 45° to the warp and weft threads. In woven cloth the warp and weft threads interweave at right angles (90°) to each other and when pulled straight, remain firm and do not stretch. When the fabric is pulled diagonally from the straight edge, the woven threads move out of place, allowing it to stretch. Therefore, if a narrow strip of fabric is cut diagonally at 45° to the woven threads (on the cross), the amount of elasticity or stretch will allow it to be manipulated around curved edges in order to lie smooth and flat. These crossway strips are used as binding or facing for neatening:

> (a) seam or hem edges.
> (b) curved raw edges, armholes and necklines.
> (c) to give a decorative finish.
> (d) when attaching collars and cuffs.

A strip or panel that is cut at any angle other than 45° to the straight thread is known as 'on the bias'. A strip on the bias will not manipulate as well as a crossway because the pull of the thread is uneven.

Bias Binding: This is a commercial name for a folded crossway strip wound on to a card which may be bought in any haberdashery department. It is available in various qualities of cotton and rayon: generally, the most suitable is one made from a fine soft cotton fabric known as nainsook. This prepared binding is particularly useful for (a) decorative finishes and (b) when crossway strips cannot be cut from the main fabric of the garment.

Dressmaking Simplified

Cutting Crossway Strips

1. Straighten two sides of the fabric to be used by cutting to a thread along both warp and weft.
2. Fold the straight warp edge across the fabric to form a right angle (90°) and parallel to the weft threads (Diagram 1).
3. Cut through the fold formed from A to B, putting the scissor blade firmly into the fold.
4. Measure in from the cut crossway edge the required width of the strip and mark with pins: a measure card is used for this. Diagram 2.
5. Cut along marked line with care as crossway moves easily out of position.

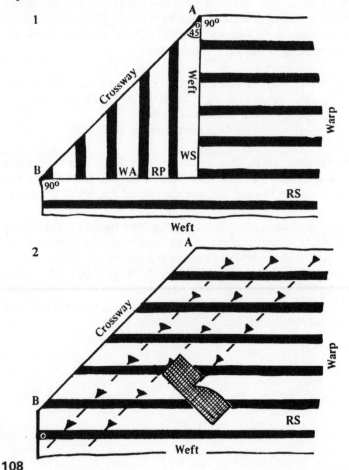

Joining a Crossway Strip

Always join crossway on the straight grain so that all seams fall in
the same direction.

1. Check that all strip ends are cut on the straight thread and in the
   same direction, i.e. all warp or all weft, forming a parallelogram.

2. Place strips in line R.S. up with straight cut ends parallel.

3. Turn strip A over on to B so that R.S. facing with the straight
   ends together. Allow a point of fabric to project 0·6 cm each side
   to give a seam allowance of 0·6 cm. Accurately positioned a right
   angled 90° will be found at points X. Pin and tack.
4. Stitch, join with 0·6 cm turnings and fasten off ends securely.
   Remove tacks. Press seam open and trim off points. If a striped
   fabric is used, plan to match stripes exactly as shown in the
   diagrams.

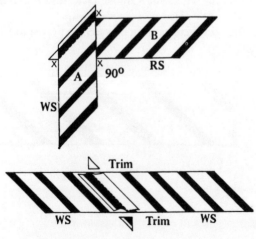

Dressmaking Simplified

Crossway Strips used for Binding

Binding may be used as a decorative method of finishing a raw edge as well as for neatening seams and raw edges on the inside of garments, particularly those of loosely woven or thick fabrics that fray easily.

The usual width of a finished bind is 0·6–1 cm but should be as narrow as possible on very fine fabrics.

General Method

1. Prepare crossway strips cut to four times finished width of bind (2·5–3·75 cm). Join one or more strips for the required length if necessary.
2. When used as an edging, trim off turning allowance on garment back to the fitting line as a bound edge neither adds nor takes away width from the cut edge. When used as a seam neatening trim turn to an even width (1·25–2 cm).
3. With R.S. facing, place edge of strip level with edge of fabric. Pin, tack and stitch 0·6 cm in from the edge. Remove tacks and press stitching. Diagram 1.
4. Turn crossway up from stitching and press smoothly upwards. Turn to W.S. and without stretching the crossway, fold over the raw edge to almost meet edge of turning and press. Diagram 2.
5. Bring folded edge over to the stitched line on W.S. and tack. Hem the fold on to the stitching. Remove tacks and press. Diagram 3.

NOTE: When bought 'bias binding' is used the prepared folds are the stitching lines.

1

WS

RS

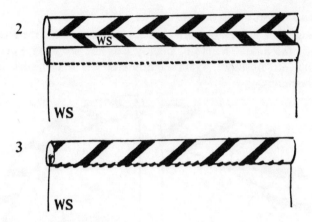

Binding Curved Edges

Follow the general method of binding (see page 110) with the following adjustments; the final result in each case should be flat, smooth and unpuckered.

Inner Curves: armholes and neck lines

The edge of a *concave* or inward curve is shorter than the stitching line for the bind; therefore, slightly *stretch* the crossway when first pinning into position. Again stretch the folded edge before final hemming.

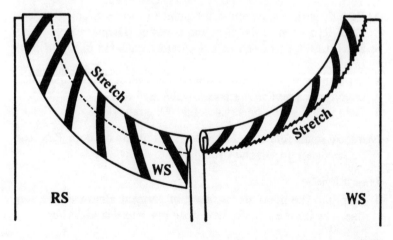

Outward Curves: shaped edges

The edge of a *convex* or outward curve is longer than the stitching line for the bind. Therefore, slightly *ease* the crossway when first pinning into position. Again slightly ease the folded edge before final hemming.

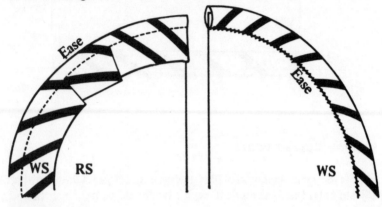

Binding Points

The binding of points and sharp angles is for decoration only, as a *shaped* facing would normally be used (see page 120). Follow the general method of binding as given on page 110 with the following adjustments.

Outward Points

1. Tack strip as far as the point and fasten thread.
2. Ease the strip back around the point to form a triangular pleat. Tack across top of the pleat and continue (Diagram 1a).
3. Stitch to the point and turn accurately, catching in top of pleat only.
4. On W.S. of point, ease in a similar small pleat to take up fullness making the point as sharp as possible and tack.
5. Hem into position on stitched line (Diagram 1b).

Note: A small fold therefore bisects the point on both R.S. and W.S. See detail on Diagram 1b.

Inward Points

1. Snip into the point across fabric of garment almost to stitching line. The inner angle can now open out into a straight line.

2. Pin, tack and stitch binding into position as method given so that the stitching is close to the base of the snip which must be stitched securely: see Diagram 2a for complete binding.
3. With angle back in position, fold garment section in half for the point with R.S. facing. Backstitch across width of bind in line with the fold. See Diagram 2c.
4. Open out flat and press this dart to one side and hem to the binding: Diagram 2b.

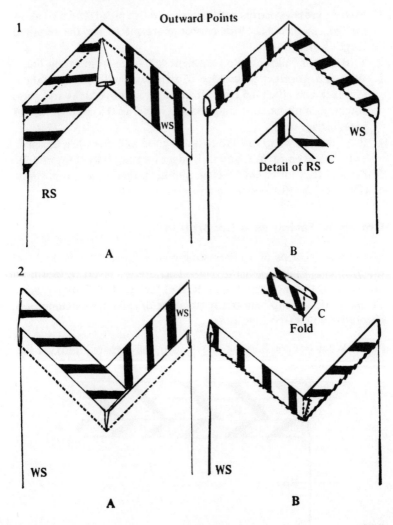

Outward Points

113

Crossway Strips used for Facing

Unless required as a decoration, crossway facings are invisible from R.S. and are used to neaten armholes, necklines and hems and in the attaching of collars and cuffs (see pages 174 and 181). If a wide facing is required, it should be a *shaped* facing (see page 120).

General Method

1. Prepare crossway strips cut to finished width plus 1·25 cm to allow for 0·6 cm turnings. Join one or more pieces for the required length if necessary.
2. Trim turning allowance on garment to 0·6 cm from fitting line.
3. With R.S. together place edge of strip level with edge of fabric. Pin, tack and stitch 0·6 cm in from edge. Remove tacks and press stitching. Without stretching crossway fold up 0·6 cm turning and press (Diagram 1).
4. Press seam turnings open to ensure a good fold line when finished. Turn facing on to W.S. and tack edge; fold carefully (Diagram 2).
5. Pin and tack lower edge facing. Slip hem, then fold into position (Diagram 2). Remove tacks and press carefully.

Crossway Facing as a Decoration

Use crossway strips of a contrasting colour applied to the R.S. of the garment. Follow general method as above, reversing position accordingly, thus at stage 3 place R.S. of facing to *W.S.* of garment. To finish, do *not* slip hem but work a line of top edge stitching as a decorative stitch (see page 103).

NOTE: When bought 'bias binding' is used, the prepared folds are the stitching lines.

Facing Curved Edges

Follow the general method of facing as given on page 114 with the following adjustments (it should be noted that these are the reverse to those for bound curves). The final result in each case should be flat and smooth.

Inward Curve: armholes and necklines

The edge stitching line of a *concave* or inward curve is shorter than the inner line of the facing. Therefore, slightly *ease* on the crossway when first pinning into position: slightly *stretch* the inner fold before slip hemming.

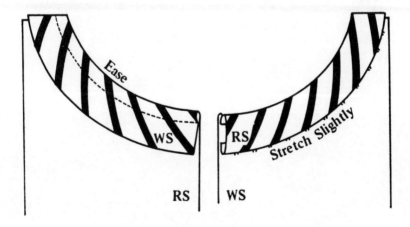

Outward Curve: shaped edges

The edge stitching line of a *convex* or outward curve is longer than the inner line of the facing. Therefore, slightly *stretch* the crossway when first pinning into position. Slightly ease in the fold before slip hemming.

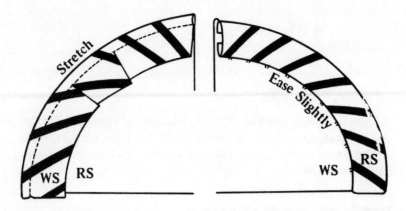

10 FACING AND INTERFACINGS

Interfacings

These are sections of firm, specifically prepared fabrics which are set into the garment to give added strength and support to areas of strain, e.g. full-length front openings with fastenings, waistbands and pockets. Interfacing also gives a firm and crisp tailored finish to collars, front openings, sleeve ends, cuffs, pocket vents and flaps.

Fabric available: from dress fabric and some haberdashery departments

Tailors canvas: Various qualities and weights suitable for use with medium to heavyweight cloth for jackets, coats and heavier weight woollen dresses.

Muslin, scrim and tarlatan: Medium and lightweight qualities suitable for dresses, blouses and lightweight jackets, some prepared as an iron-on fabric (see note below).

Bonded fabrics, i.e. non-woven: Available in medium and light weights and also as 'iron-on' fabric. These non-woven fabrics are economical as they can be cut in any direction but they do not blend so smoothly with the main fabric as does woven interfacing. Superdrape is an interfacing which has special slits running in uniform lines allowing it to move with the fabric when stretched, i.e. for use in knitted fabrics such as jersey and woollens. A transparent interfacing is available for 'see through' fabrics, voiles, lawns, etc., which ensures that the interfacing remains transparent when ironed into place.

NOTE: 'Iron on' interfacings should be used with discretion as they reduce the pliable movement and handling of the main fabric although special interfacings are manufactured for knitted fabrics.

Dressmaking Simplified

Three uses of interfacing are shown opposite. Interfacings must always be cut to the same grain as the section on which it is to be used and placed on the main fabric so that seam turnings with the added bulk fall towards the inside of the garment. For tailored collars, however, it is used on the undersection. The interfacings are basted in position on the W.S. of the fabric before making up; it is then held in place by seams or construction lines. The basting is not removed until the garment is completed. Seam turnings of the interfacing must be trimmed to 0·3 cm to reduce bulk. No turning is to be taken into a seam.

1.

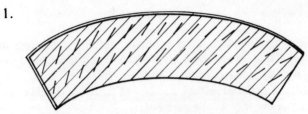

Interfacing basted on to the under collar

2.

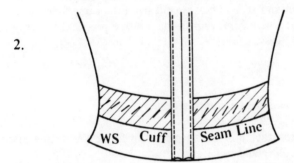

Interfacing basted into position on the cuff edge of a sleeve

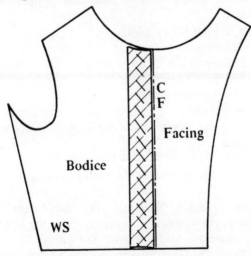

Interfacing basted into position on the bodice

Dressmaking Simplified

Shaped Facing

Shaped facings are used to finish armholes, necklines, openings and shaped edges. They are invisible except on coats and jackets and when they form a rever collar on dresses and blouses.

As a form of decoration they can be cut from contrasting fabric and applied to the R.S. of the garment.

These facings are cut as the pattern and grain of the garment but omit panel lines; the width and finished shape vary as is most suitable for the position and style. They are cut from the same fabric as the garment except where firm, thin fabric is more practical for use on thick or loosely woven fabric.

Facing on Armhole

All bodice seams must be completed.

1. With R.S. together join facing pieces on fitting line with a plain seam at shoulder and underarm.
   Press seams open and trim turnings to 1 cm.
2. Fold over 0·6 cm turning from the outer edge of the facing on to the W.S., and tack.
   Stitch 0·3 cm in from folded edge.
   Remove tacks and press.
3. With R.S. of facing to R.S. of the garment, match balance marks, fitting lines and seam lines at shoulder and under-arm.
   Pin, tack, and stitch into position. Diagram 1.
4. Trim seam turnings to 1 cm and snip into the curved seam allowance, snipping more closely at the under-arm, where it is most curved (Diagram 1).
5. Turn facing through to W.S., bringing stitched line exactly on to the fold (or very slightly towards the inside) and tack this fold into position.
   Turn garment through to W.S. and press folded edge carefully.
6. Attach the facing in position by hemming on to the turning only of shoulder, under-arm and any panel line seams.
   Remove tacks. If the fabric is very resilient and the facings are likely to 'roll' at the folded edge, one of the following alternatives should be used.

NOTE: Before turning through to W.S., press facing up from the stitched line and against the turning. Stitch the facing on to the seam allowance *only* about 0·3 cm from stitched line. Complete as above at Stage 6.

or

Turn facing through to W.S. and tack into position as Stage 5, and work a line of top stitching from the R.S. not more than 0·3 cm in from folded edge. Complete as above at Stage 6.

Armhole Facing

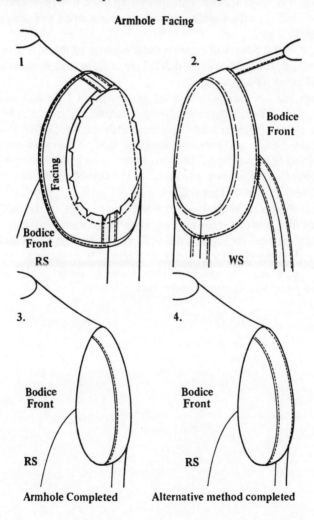

Armhole Completed   Alternative method completed

Facing a Neck Edge

The basic method is the same as that for facing an armhole. Instructions and diagrams are given for a neckline with centre back zip fastening; the same method would apply for a front neck opening. Before facing the neck, shoulder and panel lines, seams should be neatened and the opening completed.

1. With R.S. together and matching fitting lines, join front and back neck facings with a plain seam. Press seams open and trim turnings to 1 cm.
2. Fold over 0·6 cm turning from outer edge on to the W.S. and tack (*not* C.B. edge). Machine stitch 0·3 cm in from fold. Remove tacks and press. Diagram 1.
3. With R.S. of facing to R.S. of garment, pin C.F. and C.B. in position. Then, matching shoulder seams, balance marks and fitting lines, pin, tack and machine stitch the neck edge.
4. Remove tacks and press stitching and using a pad press turnings open to ensure a good fold. Trim turnings to 1 cm (0·6 cm on fine fabrics) and snip seam allowance of the curved edge and trim off corners at C.B. Diagram 2.
5. Turn facing to W.S., bring stitched line to edge of the fold and tack into position. (See note on page 121.)
6. Turn garment through to the W.S. and press edge fold carefully. Pin shoulder seams in place. Turn under C.B. edges on to the tape of the zip fastener and hem. Hem facing to turnings of shoulder and panel line seams. Remove tacks.

1. **Facing Prepared**

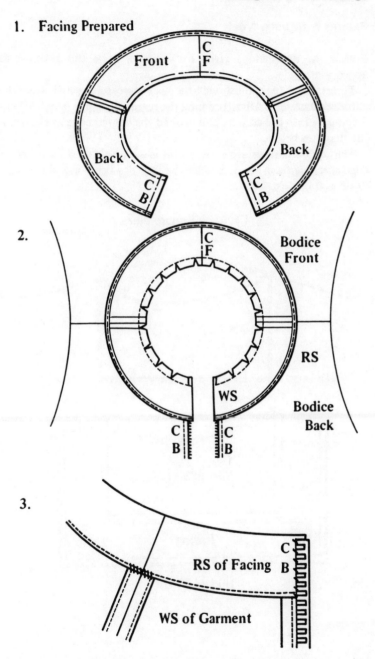

2.

3.

Facing a Square Neck

Follow the instructions given for facing a neck and armhole as appropriate.

To attain a square finish tack the neckline carefully and stitch the corners accurately. After trimming the seam allowance (stage 4) snip diagonally into the corners and around the curved edge as shown in the diagram below.

The square corners are weak and it is advisable to work a line of edge stitching from the R.S. after the fold has been tacked in place, as diagram below.

Facing a Square Neck

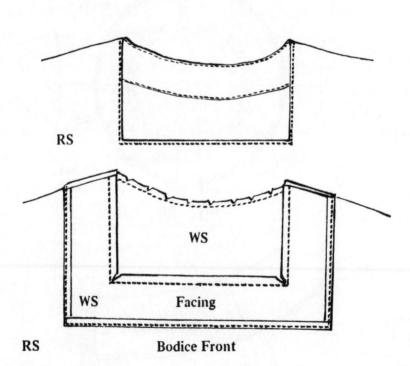

Decorative Neck Facing

Follow the basic instructions with these adjustments at:

Stage 2. Tack but do not stitch edge folded on to W.S. of facing.
Stage 3. Place the R.S. of the facing to the *W.S.* of garment. Continue as directed.
Stage 5. Turn the facing on R.S. of garment and tack fold in place. Pin seams and points correctly, then carefully pin and tack edge of facing into position.

Finish both neck edge and facing edge with a line of top stitching 0·15 cm in from the fold. Remove tacks and press. A decorative stitch can be worked instead of final top stitching (see page 230).

Decorative Neck Facing

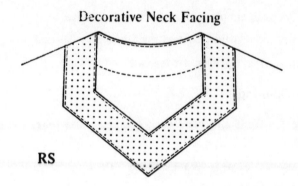

RS

11 OPENINGS

The major openings and methods of fastening are explained in the following chapter.

Blouses, lightweight dresses, lingerie and children's wear often require a small, neat opening, with a simple fastening at the edge of the garment. For example, a wrist opening in a long tight sleeve is necessary: the opening must be sufficiently long for ease in dressing and the end must be stitched strongly and accurately to withstand strain.

The choice of opening is determined by the position, purpose and fabric. They can be planned to be both practical and decorative. The three types of opening in general use are:

Faced Opening: simple, unobtrusive *or* decorative.

Bound Opening: visible, contrasting fabric may be used.

Continuous Strip Opening: strong, with underlap.

Faced Opening

Suitable for front and back neck openings, and long sleeve wrist openings.

1. Mark the position and length on the garment with a line of tacking (Diagram 1).
2. Cut out the facing: length of the opening *plus* 5 to 6·25 cm.
3. Mark out the length of the opening with tacking down the centre of the facing.
4. Neaten three raw edges with edge stitching (Diagram 2).
5. With R.S. together, place the two tacked lines directly on top of each other and tack together.
6. Starting 0·6 cm out from the tacked line, machine stitch down to the base of the line and up again 0·6 cm out at the top (Diagram 3).
7. Press, cut down the tacked line as far into the point as possible.
8. Turn the facing through to W.S. of the garment.
9. Tack the folded edge into position and press (Diagram 4).
10. Strengthen the opening by edge-stitching from R.S.

Faced Opening

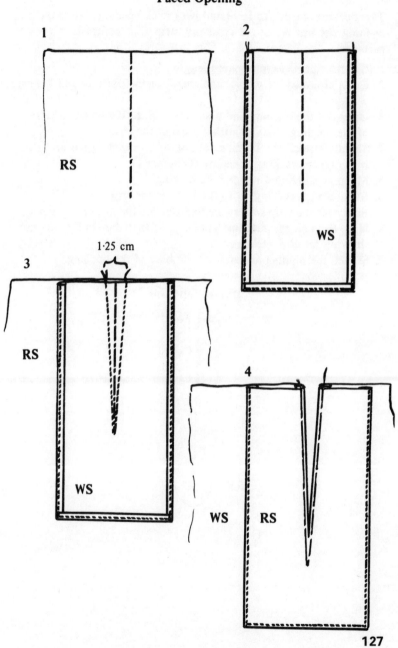

Bound Opening

This opening is used for front and back neck openings. To make the opening decorative, use a crossway strip that contrasts with the garment.

1. Cut the opening the required length.
2. Cut a crossway strip twice the length of the opening and 2·5 cm wide.
3. Open out the opening and place the R.S. of the strip to the R.S. of the opening. Tack to within 2 cm of the base.
4. Slightly stretch the binding for the following 3·75 cm and then complete the tacking as before (Diagram 1).
5. Machine stitch and remove the tacking.
6. Make 0·6 cm turning on to the W.S. of the strip.
7. Fold over the strip so that the fold touches the machine stitching.
8. Hem through the machine stitching so that the stitches do not show on the R.S. (Diagram 2)
9. Stretch the binding as before at the base of the opening.

Bound Opening

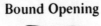

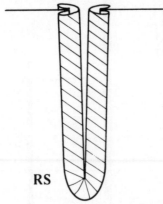

RS

Bound Opening

1

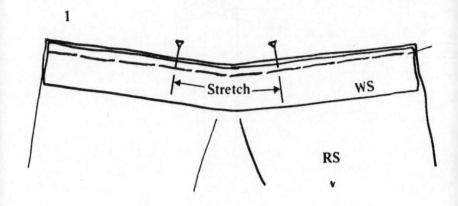

2

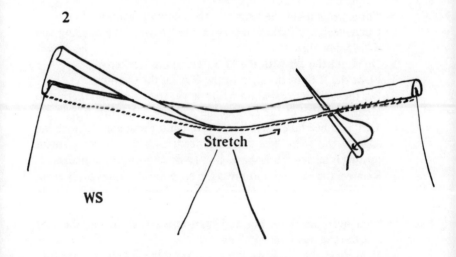

Continuous Strip Opening

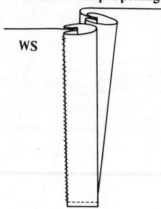

Continuous Strip Opening: suitable for lingerie

1. Cut a straight slit the length of the opening required.
2. Cut a straight of grain strip twice the length of the opening and 5–6·25 cm wide.
3. Open out the slit with the W.S. facing the worker.
4. Place the R.S. of the strip to the R.S. of the opening.
5. Pin the strip into position with the garment turning tapering to almost nothing at the base of the opening. (Diagram 1.)
6. Tack and machine stitch, with a 0·6 cm turning parallel with the edge of the strip. The stitching needs care where the garment turning is narrow at the base. It must be smooth and unpuckered.
7. Remove the tacking and press the strip and turnings away from the garment. Crease a 0·6 cm turning along the free edge of the strip.
8. Fold over the strip, pin and tack into place so that the fold touches the machine stitching.
9. Hemstitch the edge of the strip into the machine stitching. Remove the tackings and press.
10. Fold the strip into place to form under and overlap—see diagram above—and backstitch 0·3 cm from the base of the opening to strengthen it.

Continuous Strip Opening

1.

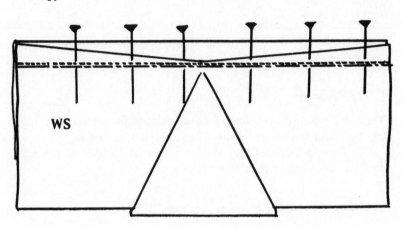

2.

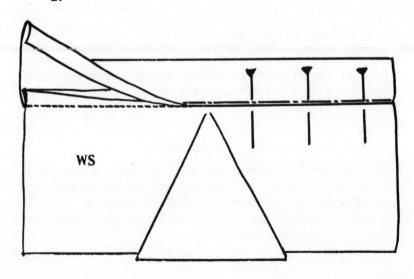

12 FASTENINGS

There are many different methods of fastening an opening. The main groups are:

1. Zip Fasteners

They are firm and neat, form a continuous edge-to-edge fastening, can be visual or inconspicuous. They are quick to fasten.

Use for top clothes only; there are various weights of zip and method according to requirements.

2. Button, Buttonholes or Loops: see page 142

A practical method except for points of strain: visual unless used in a fly opening: can be considered as part of the style of the garment and its decoration.

Use for all garments; various methods according to requirements.

3. Press Studs: see page 156

Are firm and secure for openings with little strain and are inconspicuous. Use for shoulder and neck openings on young children's wear; on wrist and similar openings and as a finish for a main buttoned opening.

4. Hooks and Eyes or Bars: see page 158

These are firm and secure under strain but strain is necessary in order that the hook and eye remain fastened. They are inconspicuous and there are various weights according to requirement.

Use for waistbands (see page 190), and as a finishing detail to a zip fastener or a buttoned opening.

General Rules for Fastenings

1. For strength the fastening must always be sewn on double fabric.
2. Unless the fastening is to be decorative, it must be as inconspicuous as possible.
3. Particular care and attention must be given to detail, accurate stitching and secure fastening on and off of the sewing thread.

Zip Fasteners

Choose the correct type and weight for the opening. The colour of the tape should match that of the garment unless a contrast is required for decoration. Types available are:

Featherweight: for neck and wrist openings.

Lightweight: for dresses, cotton skirts and shorts.

Skirt Weight: for skirts, shorts and trousers.

Open Ended: for jackets, cardigans and coats.

Curved: for front openings on trousers.

Invisible: for skirts and dresses.

Decorative: for dresses and jackets.

There are four methods of inserting a zip fastener:

1. *Visual:* for decoration only.
2. *Semi-concealed:* for neck, wrist, side and C.B. openings in lightweight fabrics for open-ended zip.
3. *Concealed:* for side C.F. and C.B. openings in dresses, skirts, shorts and trousers.
4. *Invisible:* for invisible fasteners *only.*

Visual Method: for inserting a zip into a panel without a seam

For a position where the zip forms part of the decoration, e.g. C.F. or pocket fastening.

1. Complete a faced opening following the method given on page 126 but instead of making a point, finish with a square end (Diagram 1). The width of opening should be 1·25 or 1 cm according to zip. The length of opening should be the length of zip teeth from fitting line.
2. Working from the R.S. of garment with zip closed and the top of the slider level with the fitting line, tack the zip into position, keeping the edge of the opening parallel with the teeth.
3. Attach the piping foot to the sewing machine and, working from R.S., stitch the faced opening on to the zip tape, making sure that the end corners are square (Diagram 1).
4. Turn to W.S. and oversew together the inner edges of the tape at the base of the teeth. Hem the side of the tape to the facing and loop stitch across the raw edge at base (Diagram 2).
5. Hold the lower edges of the facing in position by slip hemming on to the garment.

1.

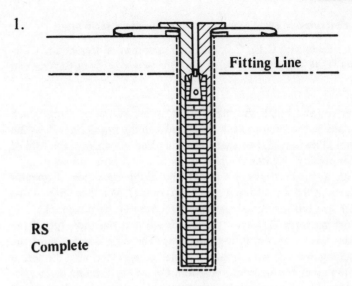

Fitting Line

RS
Complete

2.

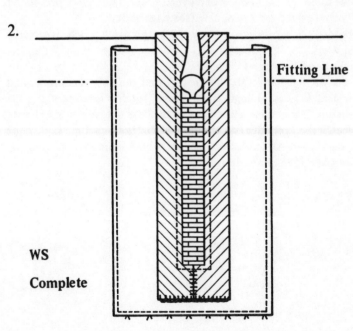

Fitting Line

WS

Complete

Semi-concealed Method: for inserting a zip into a plain seam

For positions with C.F., C.B. and side openings of dresses and over-blouses; C.B. openings on skirts and open-ended zips on jackets and coats.

1. Prepare and stitch the plain seam as far as the opening which should be the length of the zip teeth from the fitting line. Press the seam allowance flat so that the fitting line remains on the fold of open section. Neaten the raw edges of both seam and opening.
2. With a marker, tack a straight line along each side of opening 0·6 cm in from the folded edge (Diagram 1). Machine stitch along each line but not across the base (Diagram 1). Remove tacks.
3. Working from R.S. with the zip closed and the top edge of the slider level with the fitting line, place the right-hand side of the opening over the zip so that the folded edge is level with the centre of the teeth and tack into position. On a C.B. opening it is advisable to have a small hook and eye at neck edges; therefore, set zip 0.3 cm down from fitting line (see page 159).
4. Hand stitch zip in position by working a back stitch over every third stitch of the machine stitched line (Diagram 2). Complete right-hand side and fasten off.
5. Tack the left-hand side in place so that the two edges meet and conceal the zip (Diagram 2). Hand stitch as before along the machine line and backstitch across the base to give a square finish.
6. Neaten the tape edges on the W.S. as for the visual method (stage 4, page 134). Attach hook and eye at neck edge on C.B. opening (see page 159).

1.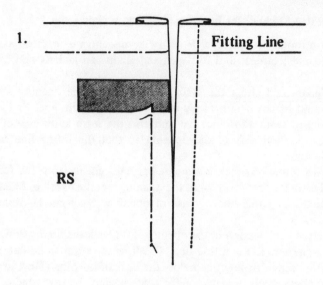

Fitting Line

RS

2.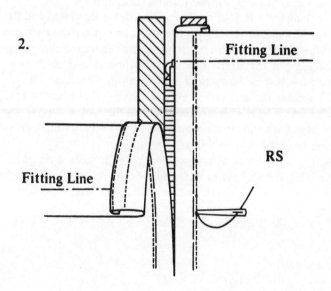

Fitting Line

Fitting Line

RS

Concealed Method: for inserting a zip into a plain seam

For positions with C.F., C.B. and side openings of dresses, skirts, shorts and trousers, and for open-ended zips on jackets and coats

1. Prepare and stitch the plain seam as far as the opening which should be the length of zip teeth from the fitting line. Press the stitched seam allowance flat and also the seam allowance of the front section *only* of the opening so that the fitting line is on the fold.
2. With a marker, tack a straight line 1·25 cm in from the folded edge on the front section of the opening, i.e. the overlap. Machine stitch along this line to base of opening (Diagram 1). Remove tacks.
3. On the back section of the opening, fold back the seam allowance 0·3 cm *beyond* the fitting line. To allow the seam to lie flat, snip across seam turning just below the base of opening (Diagram 1). Machine stitch the edge of the fold; neaten the raw edge of the seam opening and snipped turning (Diagram 1).
4. Working from R.S. of the garment with the zip closed and the top edge of the slider level with the fitting line, place the back section of the opening over the zip tape so that the folded edge is against the edge of the teeth: tack into position. Hand stitch over the machine line as the method given in stage 4 on page 136.
5. To enclose the zip, tack the front overlap into place so that the edge fold is level with the *fitting line* on the back section (Diagram 2). Hand stitch over the machined line and backstitch across the base to give a square finish (Diagram 2).
6. Neaten tape edges as the method given in stage 4 on page 134. Attach hook and eye at neck edge of C.B. opening (see page 158).

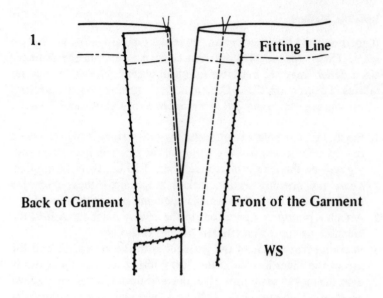

1.

Fitting Line

Back of Garment

Front of the Garment

WS

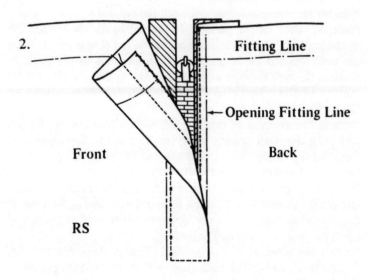

2.

Fitting Line

← Opening Fitting Line

Front

Back

RS

Invisible Method

A method used for inserting an 'invisible' type zip *only* into a plain seam. These zips are of a different construction from the ordinary zip fastener: they are available in a firm weight suitable for heavier fabrics. Position on C.F., C.B. and side openings on dresses and over-blouses and side and C.B. openings on skirts, shorts and trousers.

1. Pin and tack the plain seam including the opening. Stitch the seam to 1·25 cm above the base position of the zip: therefore, the opening will be the length of zip teeth less 1·25 cm from fitting line. *Leave* the opening section tacked but remove tacks from the stitched seam. Press the turnings open and neaten the raw edges.
2. Attach a piping or zipper foot to the sewing machine. Adjust the machine to approximately ten stitches to 2·5 cm.
3. Working from W.S. of the garment with the zip closed and the top of the slider level with the fitting line, place the zip centrally over the tacked seam line. Tack the tape firmly to the seam allowance *only* (Diagram 1). On C.B. neck openings, position the slider 1·25 cm below the fitting line.
4. Remove the seam tackings and open the zip fully.
5. Place the whole of the garment to the left-hand side so that the right-hand side of seam allowance can be flat (Diagram 2). With the teeth opened back, machine stitch as close to the teeth as possible through the tape and seam allowance only, working from the top of the opening to the top of the zip slider. Fasten off (Diagram 2).
6. Reverse the garment so that the left-hand allowance can lie flat and, with the teeth opened back, machine stitch the second side from the top of zip slider to the top end of the opening.
7. Gently and carefully close the zip fastener.
8. Position the garment as at stage 5 and, stitching through the tape and seam allowance only, stitch from 1·25 cm above the base of the zip to the end of the tape. Reverse position of garment and stitch the second side (see Diagram 3).
9. Neaten the tapes as in the method given at stage 4, page 134. Attach hook and eye at neck edge of C.B. opening (page 159).

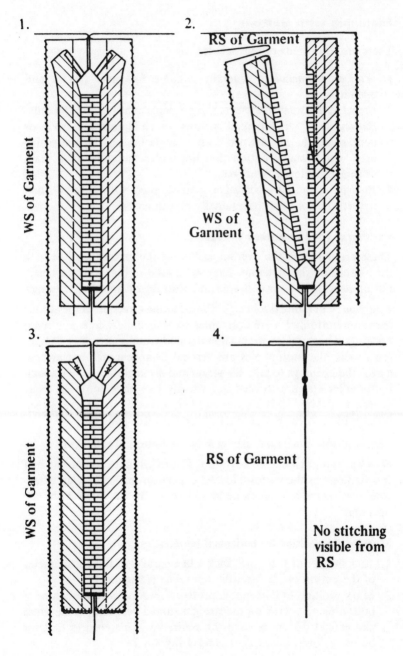

Fastening with Buttons

There are four kinds of buttonholes, viz.

1. *Worked Buttonholes:* generally suitable for most fabrics and openings.
2. *Bound Buttonholes:* for use on top garments of heavier fabrics only.
3. *Buttonhole Loops:* for small openings on children's wear, wrist or neck openings, all fastened with a single button. They are also used with a single button that lies under the collar of a main opening on blouses and coats.
4. *Rouleau Loops:* a decorative method used with several small covered buttons and occasionally on top coats.

Position of hand or worked buttonholes

These are made on the overlap section of the garment in line with the buttons on the underlap. They are placed so that when fastened, button rests on C.F. or C.B. line and centrally on all other openings.

Direction: Cut along the straight thread in the direction of the strain; therefore buttonholes are horizontal on waistbands, cuffs and main openings. On shoulder strap, shoulder and crutch openings on children's wear, the buttonholes are vertical in appearance but are cut across the openings to take the strain and are regarded as horizontal buttonholes and are worked accordingly (see page 145). On front openings of skirts, shirt blouses and light dresses where there is very little strain, *vertical* buttonholes are worked (see page 145).

Length of slit: equals the diameter of the button plus 0·3 cm.

Overlap: this must extend beyond C.F. or C.B. line at least one half the diameter of the button plus 0·3 cm (Diagram 1). Overlap extension and method of marking is the same for all other buttoned openings.

Marking the position for horizontal buttonholes:

1. Tack in C.F. or C.B. line. Tack a line parallel to this the diameter of the button inside from the centreline (Diagram 1).
2. Mark position of buttonhole slit to correspond with the centre of button placing, tack on the straight thread between parallel lines and extend 0·3 cm beyond the centreline. This ensures that the button will rest on the centreline (Diagram 2).

Marking the position for vertical buttonholes:

1. Tack in C.F. or C.B. lines and mark with a pin the position to correspond with the centre of the button.
2. Tack mark half the length of the buttonhole slit on either side of the pin (Diagram 3).

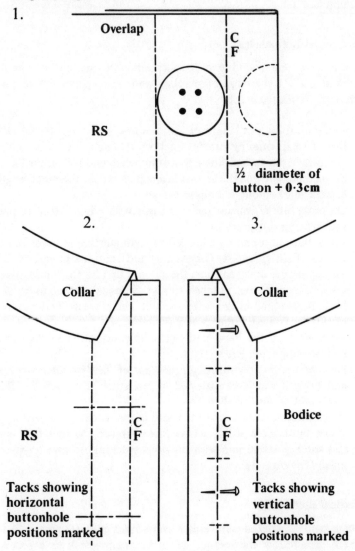

1.

Overlap

C
F

RS

½ diameter of
button + 0·3cm

2.

Collar

RS

C
F

Tacks showing
horizontal
buttonhole
positions marked

3.

Collar

Bodice

C
F

Tacks showing
vertical
buttonhole
positions marked

143

Dressmaking Simplified

Worked Buttonholes

May be used on all weights of fabric. Use buttonhole twist for medium and heavyweight fabrics. Worked buttonholes are made through double fabric, therefore facings, collars and cuffs must be completed first.

Horizontal Buttonholes

These have one round end to accommodate the button shank, worked nearest the edge of overlap, and one square end to give strength. Work from R.S.

1. Mark position and length of buttonholes; see page 143. Work a line of small running stitches (stabbed through thick fabric) 0·15 cm away from tacked line and around each end (Diagram 1).
2. Snip carefully through the two layers and cut slit the exact length of tack mark, along a straight thread.
   On loose fabric oversew the raw edges with a fine thread to prevent fraying (Diagram 2).
3. Work buttonhole stitch from left to right starting at lower inside corner of slit (point A, Diagram 3) and continue to end of slit.
4. Taking needle down through the slit and up into the fabric, oversew the round end, stitches should be equal in length to the buttonhole stitch in line with the slit. Therefore an odd number of stitches is used, either 5 or 7 (Diagram 4).
5. Turn work in the hand and buttonhole stitch the second side, still working from left to right.
6. Pass the needle down through the knot of the first stitch worked and bring it out level with end of last stitch (Diagram 5). This holds end of slit together.
7. Work three stitches across the width of the stitching (Diagram 6). Work buttonhole stitch across these threads, so that first and last stitches are in line with previous stitching, to give a square finish (Diagram 7).

Vertical Buttonholes

These can be worked with either two round ends (Diagram 8) in which case follow the method given but complete with a second round end of oversewing or with two square ends (see Diagram 6, page 155); in this case work both sides first then work square bar at each end.

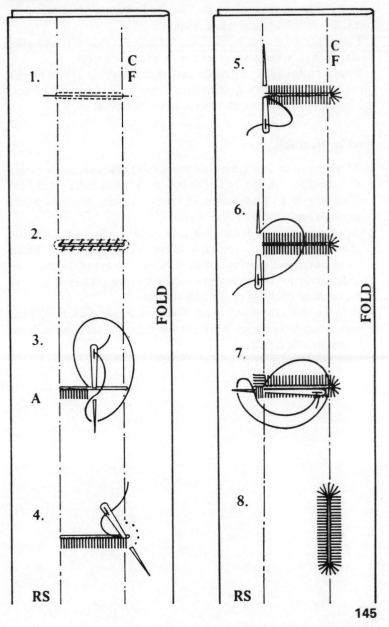

Bound Buttonholes

Used on medium and heavyweight top garments and can, if necessary, be made on the cross or bias, in which case a piece of tape must be tacked to the W.S. in preparation.

This is not a suitable method for buttonholes that will take great strain, such as waistbands or straps on children's wear.

Bound buttonholes are made first through single fabric ONLY (or fabric and interfacing when used), they are not completed until the facing has been attached and is in its final position.

Working from R.S.

1. Mark position and length of buttonhole through *single* fabric. Cut crossway binding 5 cm wide by length of buttonhole + 2·5 cm. Fold strip in half lengthwise and press. Lay the fold against the position and tack with R.S. facing.
2. Open out strip and tack through both thicknesses along the creased line. Work a rectangle of machine stitching 0·3–0·5 cm from tacked line starting one-third of the way along the long side, and making the same number of stitches across each end; finishing by working over 3–4 of the first stitches.
3. Remove tack marks and press. Fold buttonhole back in half and snip through each layer, open out and cut to 0·3 cm from each end and snip into corner.
4. Pass the binding strip through to W.S.

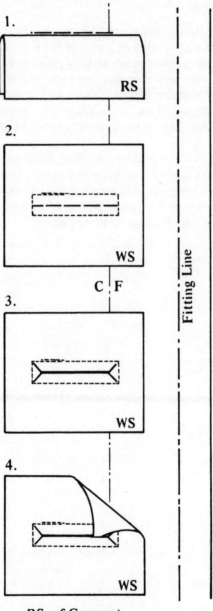

1.

RS

2.

WS

C | F

3.

WS

4.

WS

Fitting Line

RS of Garment

Working from W.S.

5. Pull the strip out flat and press. This ensures that the corners are snipped sufficiently so that strip can lie flat without puckers.
6. Place the turnings back to their original position, i.e. flat, and fold the binding strip back over them on each long side, to form an inverted pleat at each end of slit. Over-sew the folded edges outside the buttonhole slit. Tack the binding into position along the machine stitched line. If fabric is difficult to handle, stab stitch through to R.S.
7. When facing has been attached and folded into position to cover the back of the buttonholes, baste to hold in place. Cut a slit in the facing to correspond with length of the buttonholes. Turn the raw edges under with a needle and hem the facing around the bound buttonhole. Remove tacks and press.

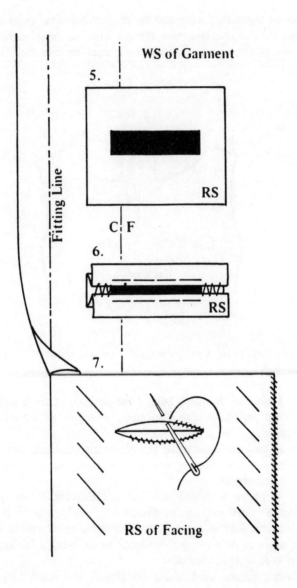

WS of Garment

5.

RS

Fitting Line

C F

6.

RS

7.

RS of Facing

Worked Loops

For use on children's wear and small openings that meet edge to edge, but do not overlap. Also for use with the small under collar button on garments with a main front opening that button up to the neck.

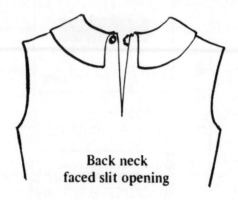

**Back neck
faced slit opening**

Use buttonhole twist. Complete neatening and garment first. Work from the R.S.

1. Place a piece of thin card behind the position of the button loop and hold in place with two pins, diameter of button apart (Diagram 1).
2. Place a third pin so that the pin *enters* the card half diameter of button away from edge of opening and bring pin up towards the edge (Diagram 2).
3. Securely fasten a thread at point C (Diagram 3) and passing behind the third pin, so that thread rests easily at point B, make stitch across fold at point A. Return in the same way to C, and back again to A, making three loops in all, work a further small stitch at A to hold thread.
4. Remove pins and card. Using the thread at A work loop stitch over the strands to finish at C. Stitches should be close and firm with the looped edge outwards (Diagrams 4 and 5).

Worked Button Loop

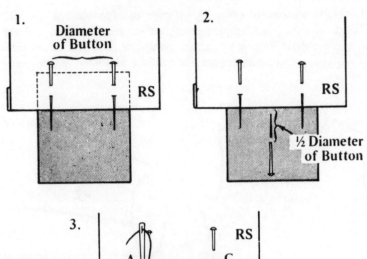

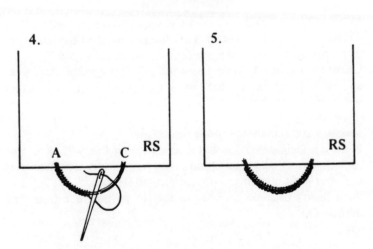

Rouleau Loops

Decorative method of fastening on edge to edge opening at C.B., C.F. or at wrists. Buttons are small, self-covered in fabric and are arranged almost touching in either groups or in a continuous line. (If required, spaced buttons may be sewn on an underlap to prevent gaping.)

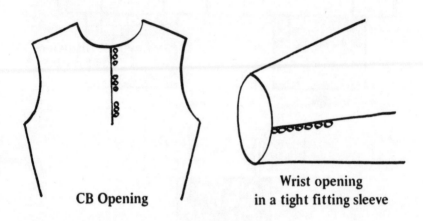

CB Opening   **Wrist opening in a tight fitting sleeve**

Rouleau button loops are made before opening is faced. Work from R.S.

1. Make sufficient length of rouleau as method given on page 219.
2. Tack the fitting line and tack a second line parallel, the diameter of button apart. Mark the position of button (Diagram 1).
3. Curve the rouleau to form loops with the seam *inside* the curve and tack into place, so that the outer edge of loop touches the width tack and allowing 0·6 cm turnings beyond fitting line (Diagram 2).
4. Machine stitch the loops along fitting line.
5. Place the facing over the loops along fitting line with R.S. together, pin tack and machine on fitting line (Diagram 3). Remove tack and press stitching. Trim turnings to 0·6 cm.
6. Turn facing back on to W.S. so that loops protrude from the folded edge.

Rouleau Loops

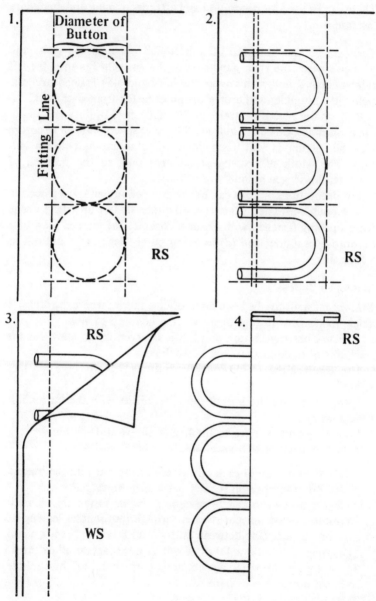

Buttons

These can be used for decoration and all types of main and secondary fastenings.

Position: on the underlap of a buttoned opening. On girls' and women's wear, the right-hand side of the garment fits over the left side: on boys' and men's wear the left-hand side fastens over the right side. Shoulder and crutch openings fasten front over back.

Buttons are placed centrally on the C.F. or C.B. lines and on all other openings. Sufficient buttons should be spaced equally to ensure that the opening is neat when closed, with no gaping between buttons. The width of spacing varies according to the position of opening, fabric weight, and size of button.

For decoration, buttons can be (a) grouped in pairs; (b) placed to give a double-breasted effect; (c) on either side of an edge-to-edge front opening fastened with either a conspicuous worked loop or a decorative braiding; and (d) as being purely decorative and not as a fastening.

Sewing on Buttons

Buttons must always be sewn on to double fabric; where the fabric is single reinforce with tape or interfacing hemmed to W.S.

A shank between button and fabric is necessary to allow for the thickness of the overwrap and buttonhole.

Use a button thread for attaching buttons that will take constant strain.

Visible holes on the button must be in line with the buttonhole (Diagram 5).

Four-hole buttons may be stitched as shown in Diagram 4.

Attach buttons after buttonholes have been worked.

1. Mark the position of each button to correspond with the buttonholes. (Button position usually marked on trade patterns.)
2. Using a double thread of matching colour fasten on securely. Work five or six upright stitches through buttonholes leaving 0·3 cm thread each time between button and fabric to form a shank (Diagram 1). On thick fabric it will be necessary to allow thread for a longer shank to accommodate thickness of buttonhole. When a button has a shank already on the underside allow for a further thread shank as necessary.

3. Before taking needle through to W.S. for the last time firmly wind thread several times around the shank (Diagram 2). On thick fabrics, when a long shank is necessary, this should be loop stitched.
4. Take thread through to W.S. and loop stitch a bar to neaten the stitches formed by sewing on button (Diagram 3). Fasten off securely.

Sewing on Buttons

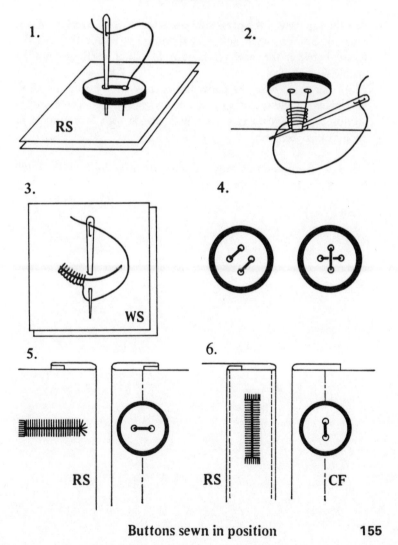

Buttons sewn in position

Press Studs

Used for openings with little strain and as a supplement to a main buttoned opening to control corner of overlap.

The section of press stud with a knob is sewn on to the overwrap so that it may be fastened by pressing down into the section with a central hole, that is sewn on the underlap (Diagrams 1 and 4). Use thread that matches the colour of garments.

1. Sew the top part of the press stud on to the W.S. of overlap. Work four stitches into each hole and slipping the needle through the fabric between the holes (Diagram 2). Stitches should not be visible from R.S.
2. Mark the position of the underpart of stud by pressing the knob into place on the underlap to make an impression. Place under-section centrally over this mark and sew on with four stitches in each hole as before.

NOTE: Larger press studs may be sewn on with buttonhole stitch (Diagram 3) using buttonhole twist.

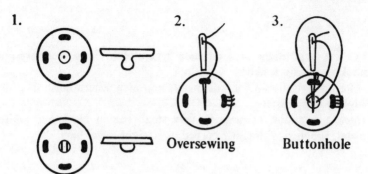

1.
2. Oversewing
3. Buttonhole

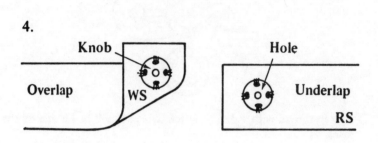

4.

Knob

Hole

Overlap

WS

Underlap

RS

Hooks and Eyes

For use in positions of strain as a degree of strain is necessary for hook to remain fastened.

Particularly useful for waistbands and as a secure finish at neck edge of a zip fastener.

Hooks: Available in large to very small size in black and white metal, supplied with either curved or straight metal bars.

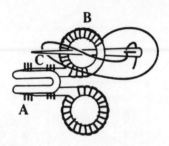

1. Fasten thread with a double stitch, where it will be hidden by the hook.
2. Place bend of hook 0·3 cm in from edge of opening and sew in position with 3 straight stitches under the actual hook, point A.
3. Slip needle through fabric to the ring and work buttonhole around each ring, point B.
4. Finish with 3 straight stitches across centre of hook between rings and 'hump' under the hook point C. Fasten off.

NOTE: Special skirt hooks, flat and strong, are available for waistbands of skirts, shorts and trousers.

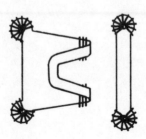

Curved metal eyes: for use on edge-to-edge fastening (Diagram 2). The loop must extend 0·3 cm beyond edge of opening, placed to correspond with hook. Work buttonhole around each ring and three straight stitches across centre.

Straight metal eyes: for use on overlapped fastening (Diagram 1). Bar is placed 0·3 cm beyond fitting line to correspond with hook. Work buttonhole stitch around each ring.

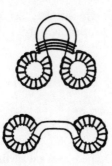

Worked Bar: neat and less conspicuous, used in place of metal eyes with small or very small hooks. Bar is made either on folded edge (Diagram 3) or on fitting line.

Work a loop stitched bar over three straight stitches, width required to take hook (see page 150).

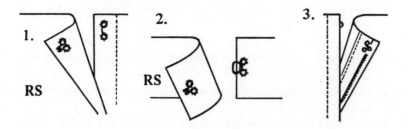

13 POCKETS

It is essential that a pocket is strongly made and large enough for its purpose. It must be firmly attached to avoid strain on the garment. Pockets are both decorative and functional, unless concealed in a seam.

Two general methods are shown: (a) Patch pockets—entirely visible; (b) Welt pockets—opening only is visible.

Patch Pockets

The pocket is formed by top stitching a 'patch' of fabric on to the R.S. of the garment.

The top edge is neatened by:

(a) Turning a plain hem approx. 1·25 cm on to W.S. and hemming in place.
(b) Turning a plain or shaped hem on to the R.S. and top stitching the hem in place, styles such as Diagrams 2 and 3.
(c) Attaching a straight or shaped facing of self fabric on or of a contrasting decorative fabric (Diagrams 2 and 3).

To apply a facing follow general methods on page 114 and place R.S. of facing to W.S. of pocket, matching fitting lines of top edge, and tack and machine stitch. Remove tacks, press stitching and turnings, open and trim to 0·6 cm (Diagram 4).

Turn facing to R.S. and turn under 0·6 cm along lower edge, tack into position and top stitch.

To attach pocket:

1. Complete the top edge as required.
2. Fold turnings of pockets to W.S. on fitting line and tack. Trim turnings to 0·6 cm. On square corners and points pleat as in Diagram 5a, on curved edges snip turnings to reduce bulk (Diagram 5b).
3. Matching balance marks, place the pocket in position on the garment and tack.
4. Following one of the methods shown in Diagrams 1, 2 and 3, start machine stitching where indicated by arrow and work support of corner first, proceed around edge of pocket to finish with the support of second corner.

Patch Pockets

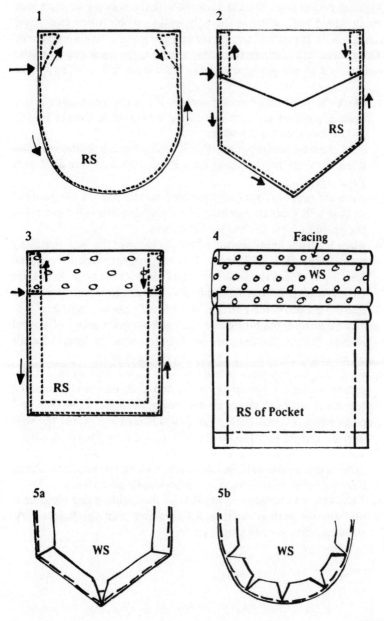

Welt Pocket

This is a pocket inset into the garment with the opening strengthened by an added welt, which is the only section visible when completed (Diagram 4). It may be inset on the straight grain or at an angle to it. The pocket bag is made from two sections, the back cut from the same fabric as the garment and the front from a fine lining fabric.

1. Mark the position of pocket mouth, if not on the straight grain, baste a piece of tape on interfacing to the W.S. Pocket mouth should be at least 9 cm wide.
2. Fold the welt in half lengthwise R.S. together, tack and machine stitch the ends on the fitting line. Press, trim and turn R.S. out. Press again.
3. Tack the prepared welt into position on the R.S. of the garment so that welt faces downwards and the fitting line is 0·5 cm *below* the position mark for the pocket mouth.
4. Place the front lining section of the pocket over the welt, matching fitting lines. R.S. of lining to R.S. of garment, tack through all four layers. Place the back section of the pocket above the pocket mouth with R.S. together and tack into position with the fitting line 0·5 cm *above* the position mark for the pocket mouth.
5. Machine stitch the fitting line each side to exact width of pocket mouth. Ensure that lines are parallel and equal in length. Fasten off all ends very securely. Remove tacks and press.
6. Fold the pocket mouth in half and snip on the fold, open out and cut to within 0·6 cm of the ends and then diagonally into the corners. Turn both pieces of the pocket through to the W.S. and press seams so that each piece hangs downward. Press the welt into an upright position on the R.S. to hide the pocket mouth.
7. Tack the front and back of the bag together making them the same width as the welt. Machine stitch along the tack line. Press, trim the turnings to 0·6 cm and neaten with oversewing.
8. Tack welt into position of the R.S. of the garment and blind hem or over-sew both ends from R.S. making both top points very strong as they take the most strain.

Welt Pocket

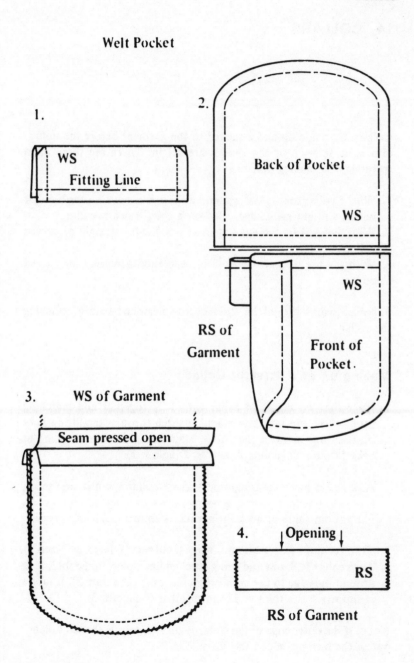

1.

WS
Fitting Line

2.

Back of Pocket

WS

WS

RS of
Garment

Front of
Pocket.

3. WS of Garment

Seam pressed open

4. Opening

RS

RS of Garment

14 COLLARS

Collars are made up and attached to the garment before the under-arm seam is sewn or the sleeves are set in. There are three main methods of attaching collars:

1. With a collar that is self neatening. This is always a simple collar with a straight neck edge, used on a shirt styled neckline.
2. With the use of a facing, a method suitable for straight or curved collars.
3. With the use of a crossway strip, a method generally for curved collars.

Shoulder seams should be stitched and neatened before attaching the collar.

Making up of a Straight Collar

1. Place the two pieces of collar with R.S. together and matching fitting lines. Pin tack and machine stitch through the fitting lines on the three sides of the collar, start and finish the stitching at neck fitting line (points A and B, Diagram 1).

    Alternative method (Diagram 2) where collar is cut in one piece, fold R.S. together matching fitting lines and stitch end lines only, likewise finishing at neck fitting line. Remove tacks and press.

2. Trim turnings to 0·3 cm and trim off corners (Diagrams 1 and 2).
3. Turn collar R.S. out and bring stitched line up on to the fold, tack around the edge to the neck fitting line only (Diagram 3). If fabric is slippery baste the two layers together (Diagram 3).

NOTE: If the outer edge of the collar is curved, snip V-shaped notches out of the turnings along the curve.

1.

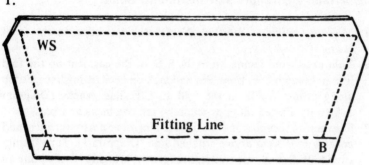

WS

Fitting Line

A   B

2.

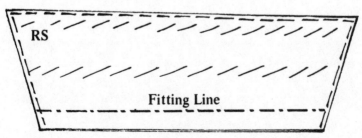

WS

Fitting Line

A   B

3.

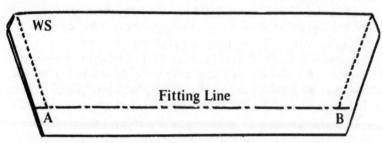

RS

Fitting Line

Dressmaking Simplified

To Attach a Straight Self-neatening Collar

1. Make up collar as directed. Neaten the raw edge on the front facing.
2. Fold each front facing on to the R.S. of the garment on the fold line and match C.F. lines. Pin and tack on neck fitting lines. Stitch along fitting line from the fold to C.F. line exactly (Diagram 1 A to B). Fasten off ends securely, remove tacks and press.
3. Snip across turnings at C.F. lines (Point B) and trim turnings and corners to 0·3 cm above stitched line (Diagram 1). Turn facings over to W.S. and ease out corners gently, bringing stitched line on to the fold and press (Diagram 2).
4. With upperside of collar against the W.S. of bodice, place edges of collar to the C.F. lines. Fold turnings of under collar away towards worker. Matching neck fitting lines of bodice and upper collar only, pin, tack, and machine stitch (Diagram 3). (If necessary ease garment on to collar.) Fasten off ends securely, remove tacks and press. Trim turnings to 0·6 cm and snip where necessary.
5. Turn the collar up and over turnings. Press collar up from the stitched line so that turnings are enclosed.
6. Working from the R.S. of garment, fold under the turnings of the under collar and lay the folded edge along the stitched fitting line, so that all turnings are inside, pin and tack into position. Hem the fold on to the machine stitching. Remove all tacks and press.

NOTE: When collar is folded in to place, the hemming is concealed.

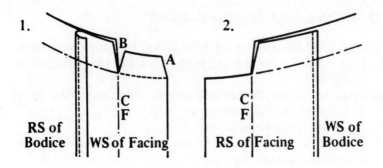

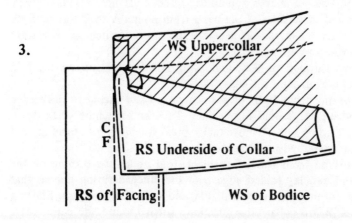

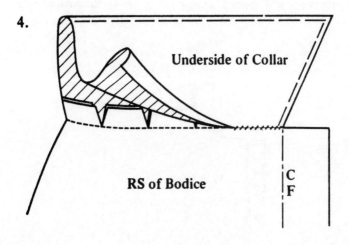

To Attach a Shirt Collar with a Band

1. Neaten the raw edge of the front facing. Fold each front facing onto W.S. of garment along the fold line and tack into position (Diagram 1).
2. Baste interfacing to the underside of collar and make up as directed for a straight collar (page 165).
3. Baste interfacing to band facing.
4. With R.S. together pin band to underside of collar matching C.B. and balance marks.
5. R.S. together, pin band facing to band, over the collar matching C.B. balance marks and fitting lines. Tack and machine stitch around three sides of the band from points A to B leaving neck edge free (Diagram 2). Remove tacks, press stitching, trim seam and snip where necessary.
6. Turn through to R.S. and bring stitched line up on the fold and tack around the edge.
7. Working from W.S. of garment, pin band facing to neck edge matching C.B. and fitting lines. Tack and machine stitch down neck fitting line. Remove tacks, press stitching, trim turnings and snip curved edges (Diagram 3).
8. Working from R.S. of garment, fold under the turning on the band and lay folded edge over the stitched fitting line so that the turnings are enclosed. Pin and tack into position. Starting at C.B. on collar edge, machine stitch around the band, overlapping the stitching for $\frac{1}{4}''$ at join (Diagram 4). Remove all tacks and press.

1.

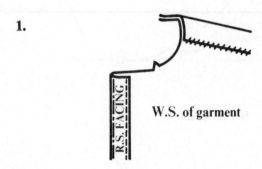

W.S. of garment

R.S. FACING

2.

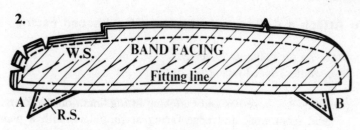

3.

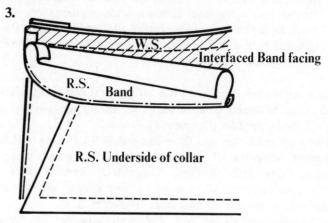

4.

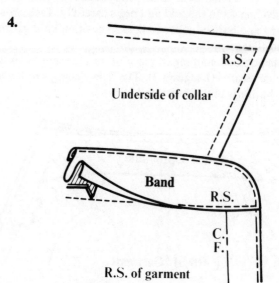

To Attach a Collar with the Use of a Shaped Facing

1. Make up the collar as directed.
2. Prepare the shaped facing:

   (a) With R.S. together and matching fitting lines, join back neck and front neck and edge facing at shoulders, with a plain seam; trim turnings and press open (on full length openings a further join in the front facing is often required).
   (b) Neaten the outer edge of the facing all round by folding 0·6 cm turnings to the W.S. Tack, machine stitch, close to the fold. Remove tacks and press.

3. Place under side of collar to R.S. of garment and bring edges to C.F. lines. Matching balance marks and fitting lines pin and tack the collar in position (Diagram 1).
4. Place prepared facing over the collar with R.S. of facing to R.S. of garment. Matching all balance marks and fitting lines pin, tack and machine stitch all round (Diagram 2). Remove tacks and press. Trim turnings to 0·6 cm, trim off corners and snip into seam allowance of the curved neck edge (Diagram 2).
5. Fold facing over to the W.S. and gently ease out the corners. Bring stitched line on to the fold and press carefully. Tack around edge of facing and base of collar to hold in position until garment is completed (Diagram 3).
6. Secure the facing by hemming in place on to the seam allowance of the shoulder seams (Diagram 3). The front facing will be held in place by buttons, buttonholes and hem.

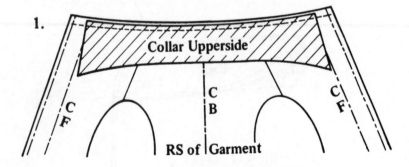

2.

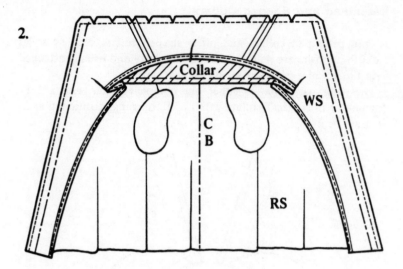

3.

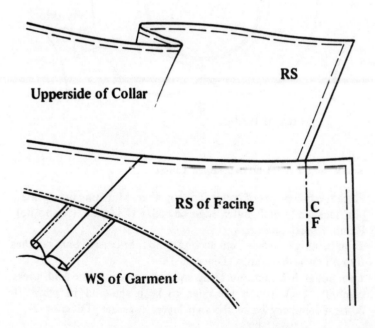

171

Peter Pan and Shaped Collars

Round peter pan collars and other shaped collars such as styles a and b opposite are made up in the same way and usually attached with the use of a crossway strip (see next page).

The peter pan collar is either one complete collar with a C.F. opening or in two half collars with a C.B. opening, positioned as in diagram below.

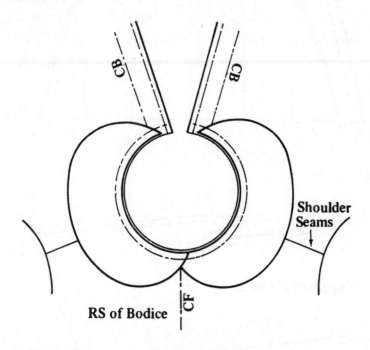

To make up a Peter Pan or Shaped Collar

1. Place the two pieces of collar R.S. together. Matching fitting lines, pin, tack and stitch outer edge of collar (Diagram 1 opposite). Remove tacks and press.
2. Trim turning to 0·6–0·3 cm according to fabric used. Snip notches into all curved turnings (Diagram 1).
3. Turn collar R.S. out and bring stitched line on to the fold, press carefully. Tack round the edge to keep the fold in place. If fabric is slippery baste the two layers together (Diagram 2).

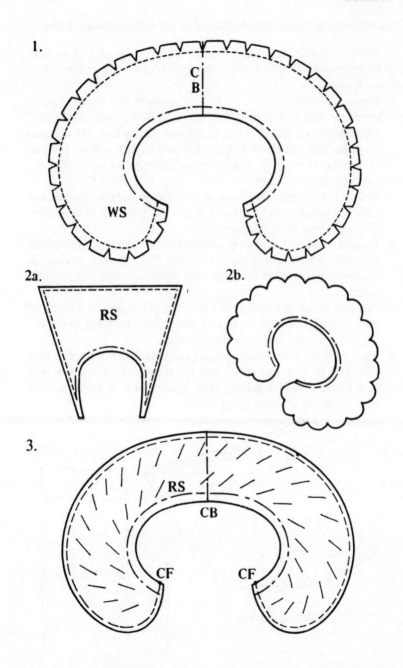

1.

C
B

WS

2a.

RS

2b.

3.

RS
CB

CF   CF

To Attach a Collar with the Use of a Crossway Strip

1. Make up collar as directed. Neaten the raw edge of C.B. or C.F. facing extension. Cut a crossway strip 2·5 cm wide and length of neck edge.
2. Place underside of collar to R.S. of garment and bring edges to meet C.F. and C.B. lines. If two half collars, are used, they should meet exactly on the C.F. line at the neck fitting line. See diagram on page 172. Match all balance marks and fitting lines, pin and tack collar in position, easing the bodice on to the collar if necessary (Diagram 1 below).
3. Fold on the extension lines and turn facing back on to R.S. and over the collar, matching centre lines. Pin and tack into position at neck fitting line (Diagram 2).
4. Place R.S. of crossway strip over collar and garment, placing the raw edge 0·5 cm above the fitting line. Pin and tack so that the crossway overlaps the facing at each side by at least 1·25 cm (Diagram 2).
5. Machine stitch from edge of extension (Diagram 2). Fasten off ends securely, remove tacks and press. Trim turnings to 0·6 cm, trim corners and snip into curved edges.
6. Turn strip up from stitched line and press. Turn strip and edge facing on to W.S. and gently ease out the corners. Crossway strip now forms a narrow facing. Tack against base of collar to hold edge of facing in place (Diagram 3).

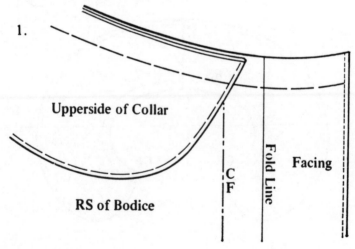

1.

Upperside of Collar

RS of Bodice

C F

Fold Line

Facing

7. Turn under 0·6 cm along raw edge of the crossway strip and, allowing this fold to stretch slightly, pin and tack the crossway flat on to the garment (Diagram 3).

   Starting at point A hem the neatened edge of the facing on to the crossway, then continue to hem the edge of the crossway in place. To finish hem second facing to crossway (Diagram 3). Remove tacks and press.

Attaching the Collar

2.

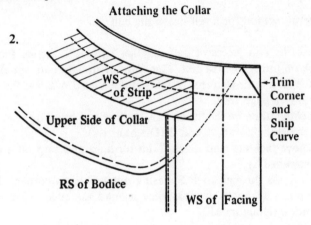

3.

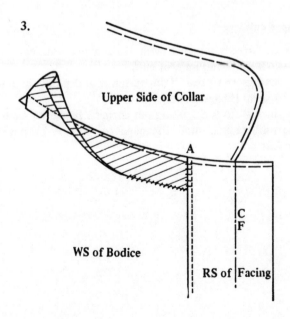

15 CUFFS

Cuff with an Overlap

A general method for a self-neatening cuff.

1. Place the two pieces of cuff together with R.S. facing. Pin and tack on fitting lines of cuff. This form of straight cuff can also be made from a single piece of fabric folded lengthways as for waist band (see page 189).
2. Machine stitch on the fitting line, starting and finishing exactly on the wristline points A and B (Diagram 1A).
3. Remove tackings and press. Trim turnings and snip off corners (Diagram 1A).
4. Turn cuffs through to R.S. easing out points on corners. Bring the seam up on to the fold, tack around the edge to keep it in position (Diagram 1B).

Open or shaped cuff

1. Place the two pieces together with R.S. facing. Pin, tack and machine stitch on fitting lines of cuff.
2. Remove tackings and press. Trim turnings and points and snip into curved seam (Diagram 2A).
3. Turn cuff through to R.S., easing out corners. Bring the seam up on to the fold, tack around the edge to keep it in position (Diagram 2B).

Making a Cuff

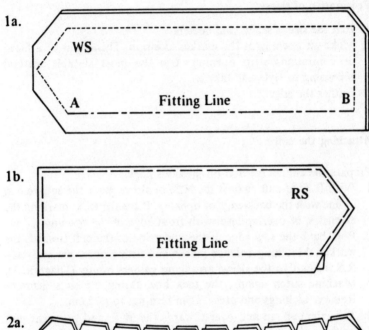

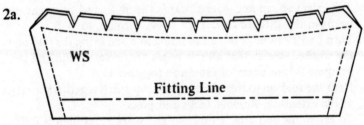

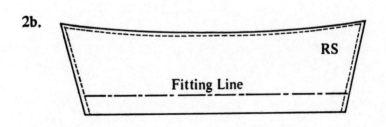

To attach a Self-neatening Cuff with Overlap

Preparation of sleeve

1. Join the sleeve seams and neaten.
2. Make an opening at the marked position. This could be a faced or continuous strip opening. Use the most suitable method according to style and fabric.
3. Gather the edge.

Attaching the cuff

Prepare the cuff as method on previous page.
1. With R.S. of cuff against the R.S. of sleeve place the square end in line with the back edge of opening. Place the tack, marking the extension of overlap level with front edge of the opening.
2. Fold back the raw edge of the underside of the cuff towards the worker. Matching balance marks and fitting lines, pin and tack R.S. of cuff to the sleeve arranging gathers evenly (Diagram 1).
3. Machine stitch against the tack line, fasten off ends securely. Remove tackings and press. Trim turnings to 1·25 cm.
4. Turn the cuff up and over towards the W.S. and press the cuff up from the stitched line. Turn sleeve through to W.S.
5. Turn under raw edge of cuff to fitting line and bring the fold on to the stitched line so that all raw edges are enclosed. Pin and tack, bringing folded edges of extension together also.
6. Hem the fold on to the stitching and slip stitch together the edges of the extension. Remove tacks and press.
7. To fasten the cuff attach a button and work a buttonhole following directions given on page 144.

Attaching a Self-neatening Cuff

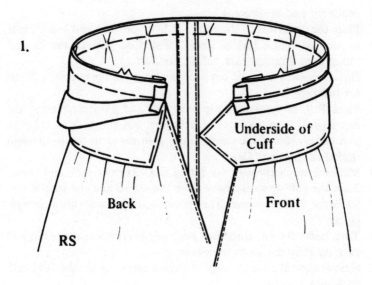

1.

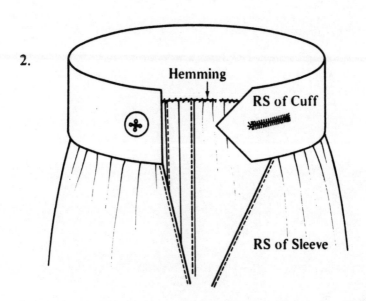

2.

To Attach a Cuff with the Use of a Crossway Strip

1. Make up cuff as directed.
2. Place the underside of the cuff to R.S. of garment and bring edges to meet at centre line of sleeve. Match all balance marks and fitting lines. Pin and tack cuff in position.
3. Cut a crossway strip 2·5 cm wide the length of the cuff + 1·25 cm for turnings.
4. Place R.S. of crossway strip over cuff and garment placing the raw edge 0·5 cm above the fitting line. Pin and tack so that the join lies on top of the sleeve seam. Join the strip on the straight thread as shown in Diagram 1.
5. Machine stitch through the fitting line. Remove tack and press.
6. Turn the cuff upwards away from the sleeve and the strip down on to the W.S. of sleeve. The crossway strip now forms a narrow facing.
7. Turn under 0·6 cm along raw edge of the crossway strip, pin and tack the strip flat on to the sleeve.
8. Hem around the tacked edge. Remove tacks, press, and fold cuff back into position.

Attaching a Cuff using a Crossway Strip

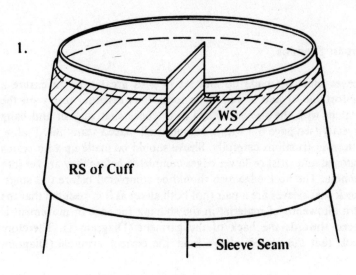

1.

WS

RS of Cuff

← Sleeve Seam

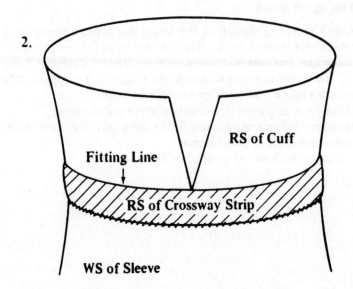

2.

Fitting Line

RS of Cuff

RS of Crossway Strip

WS of Sleeve

16 SLEEVES

Set-in Sleeves

Sleeves must be made up and set in with great care, to ensure a comfortable fit and a well-made look. It is essential to try on the garment with the sleeves tacked in to check that they fit and hang correctly (see page 61) with a smooth well-placed seam line. Follow pattern instructions carefully. Sleeve should be made up with seams neatened and wrist or lower edges completed *before* they are set into armhole. The neck edge also should be completed before this stage. Check that sleeves are a pair (not both alike) as it is essential that the extra allowance of material in the shaping for ease of movement is placed towards the back of the garment (Diagram 1). Therefore check that the correct sleeve is in the correct armhole (Diagram 2).

Making up the Sleeve

1. Run a gathering thread on the fitting line around sleeve head between the balance marks. Run a second thread 0·3 cm above the fitting line. For ease in drawing up even disposal of fullness, work this line in the opposite direction (see Diagram 1). (Approx. 3·75 cm extra fabric is allowed for ease of movement.)
2. Make darts at elbows if necessary and press downwards.
3. Matching balance marks and fitting lines, pin, tack and finish under-arm seam or panel seams.
4. Complete the lower or wrist edge. See Chapter 15.

Sleeves

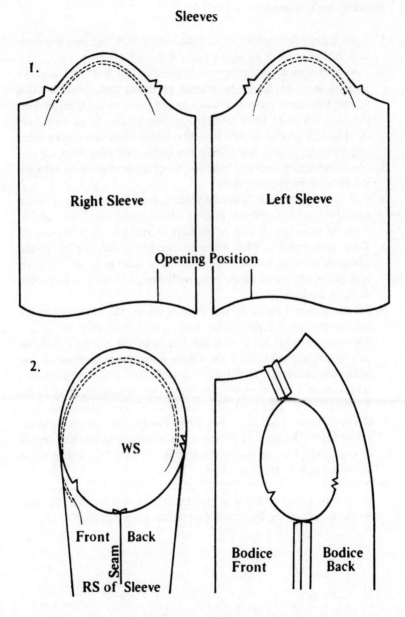

1.

Right Sleeve

Left Sleeve

Opening Position

2.

WS

Front | Back

Seam

RS of Sleeve

Bodice Front

Bodice Back

Sleeve RS out and bodice WS out ready for assembly

Setting in a Sleeve

1. Turn bodice through to W.S., place sleeve R.S. out into the arm-hole (therefore R.S. of sleeve faces R.S. of bodice).
2. Match and pin the balance marks, the shoulder line mark and the under-arm seam. In more tailored garments and those in thick fabrics the sleeve seam is usually placed towards the front bodice, this avoids a bulky seam intersection. Work with the garment held so that the worker looks into the sleeve with the sleeve head uppermost. Pin and stitch from the sleeve side (Diagram 1).
3. Matching fitting lines pin together the under-arm sections between the balance marks and tack.
4. Pull up the gathering threads until the sleeve head fits the armhole and disperse the gathers evenly. Matching fitting lines, pin at frequent intervals so that no gathers or tucks form (Diagram 1).
5. Tack with small stitches through the fitting line easing in the gathered section. As the edge of a sleeve head is on the cross or bias grain, the extra fabric can, with care, be eased in smoothly without puckers.
6. Try the garment on for fit and hang of sleeve. Make any necessary adjustments or alterations. See section on fitting, page 61.
7. Turn the garment back over the sleeve to the same position as before (Diagram 1). With the sleeve uppermost machine on the fitting line starting 2·5 cm from the under-arm seam; stitch across seam, around the armhole and across under-arm seam to finish 2·5 cm beyond. This strengthens a point of strain (Diagram 2).
8. Remove tacks and press stitching. Press seam turnings, open sleeve head (Diagram 2) by using a pad and damp cloth to shrink in ease (see pressing instructions pages 16 and 18). This gives a smooth finish to the seam line.
9. Allow turnings to come together again and trim evenly to 1·25 cm. Neaten by either machine or hand stitching or with a fine binding as the details given for armhole neatening on page 98.

Setting in a Sleeve

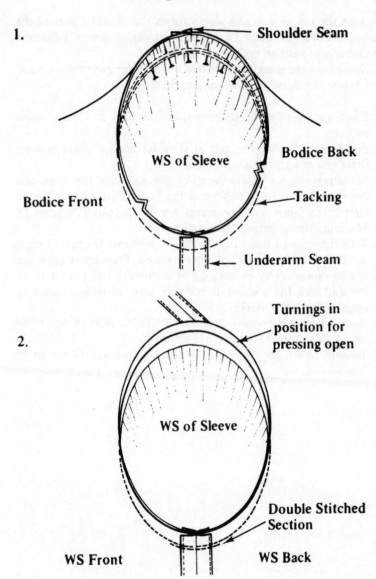

1.

Shoulder Seam

WS of Sleeve

Bodice Back

Bodice Front

Tacking

Underarm Seam

2.

Turnings in position for pressing open

WS of Sleeve

Double Stitched Section

WS Front

WS Back

Raglan Sleeve

Because the top of a raglan sleeve forms the shoulder part of the bodice, the order of making a garment with raglan sleeves is different to that of one with an ordinary armhole.

The sleeve head is set in *before* side seams of the garment are made and *before* the sleeve is made up and finished.

1. Stitch and finish darts, style lines, etc., on back and front bodice sections.
2. Pin, tack and stitch the dart at shoulder line on sleeve section. Press and neaten as shown on page 73.
3. Matching balance marks carefully pin and tack the front and back armhole seams to those of the bodice, taking care not to stretch the fabric as these seams are on the bias (Diagram 1). Machine stitch, remove tacks and press.
4. Trim the seam turnings to 1·25 cm and snip into the curved edges to allow turnings to lie flat when pressed. Press seam open and neaten raw edges by overcasting or loop stitch (see page 97).
5. Pin and tack the under-arm and side seam of bodice matching seam and balance marks.
6. To strengthen the seams at under-arm, tack a piece of tape to the fitting line around the curve (Diagram 2).
7. Machine stitch the seam. Remove tacks, press and neaten as the armhole seams.

Raglan Sleeve

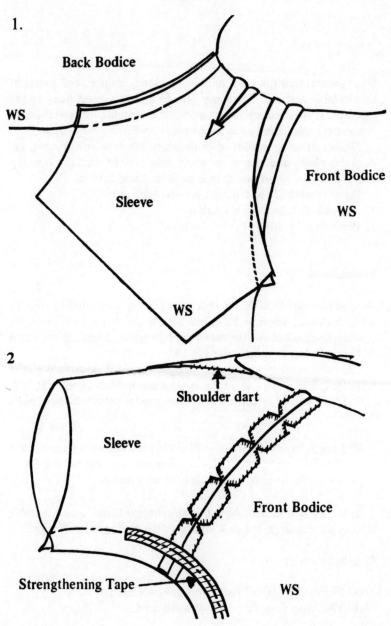

1.

Back Bodice

WS

Sleeve

Front Bodice

WS

WS

2

Shoulder dart

Sleeve

Front Bodice

Strengthening Tape

WS

17 WAISTBANDS and BELTS

It is essential that the waist finishes on skirts, trousers and shorts fit comfortably and are sufficiently firm to ensure a good hang to the garment. It is necessary to use a strong interlining or petersham to prevent the waistband stretching as it is under constant strain.

The waistline is finished *after* the skirt has been constructed, i.e. pockets, pleats and seams neatened and pressed and the opening completed, but *before* the hem is measured and turned.

The two methods of finishing a waist edge are:
1. Applied waistband of self fabric.
2. Petersham set inside top of skirt.

Waistband

To obtain a good finish it is necessary for the waistband to overlap when fastened; this can be either with a pointed extension of the overlap (method shown in detail over page), or a square extension of the underlap as shown on page 192.

The band must be cut on the straight thread if possible with the selvedge grain lengthwise, as this is stronger and less easily stretched.

Cut the band as directed by the commercial pattern if used, or as follows:

(a) Length required—which is firm waist measurement plus 2·5 cm plus 3·75 cm allowance for overlap plus 1·25 cm turnings ×
(b) Twice the finished width plus 1·25 cm turnings.

The interlining also must be cut on the straight thread; use a suitable interlining, see page 117 or a strong calico or bonded stiffening.

Cut the interlining—

(a) Finished length of band plus 0·6 cm turnings ×
(b) The *exact* finished width of waistband.

Making Waistbands

1. Mark the fold line clearly, also fitting line and shape of overlap if pointed.
2. Baste the interfacing into position.

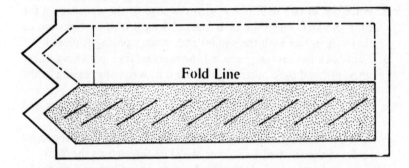

3. Fold in half lengthwise, R.S. together.
4. Tack and stitch each end exactly on the fitting line, *not* across turnings. Press. Trim end turnings and point closely.

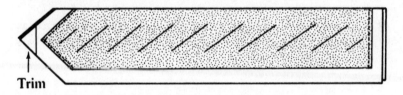

5. Turn band through to R.S. easing out point and corners.

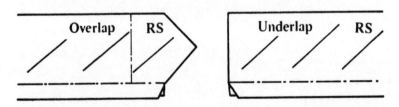

6. The same method is used for preparing square ended band with underlap extension.

Setting on Waistband

Pointed Extension of Overlap:

1. With the fold of the band towards the hem, place the R.S. together, the stiffened side of the band against the R.S. of the skirt.
2. Place the square end in line with the edge of the opening on the back of skirt. Place the tack marked length of the extension, so that it is in line with the square end, when opening is closed.
3. Fold back the raw edge nearest the marker, then matching fitting lines, pin and tack outer edge of band to waist line, easing in the skirt if necessary (Diagram 1).
4. Machine stitch against the tacked line, remove the tackings and press. Trim skirt turning to 1·25 cm.
5. Lift the band up and over towards the W.S. and press the band *up* from the stitched line. Turn the skirt through to the W.S.
6. Fold under the raw edge of the band to fitting line and bring the fold down to machine stitching, so that all raw edges are enclosed. Pin and tack.
7. Hem the folded edge on to the machine stitching and slip stitch together the straight edge of the extension. Remove tacks and basting. Press.
8. Complete the waistband with three hooks and bars placed as shown in Diagram 2. For method of attaching hooks and bars see page 158.

Setting on Waistband

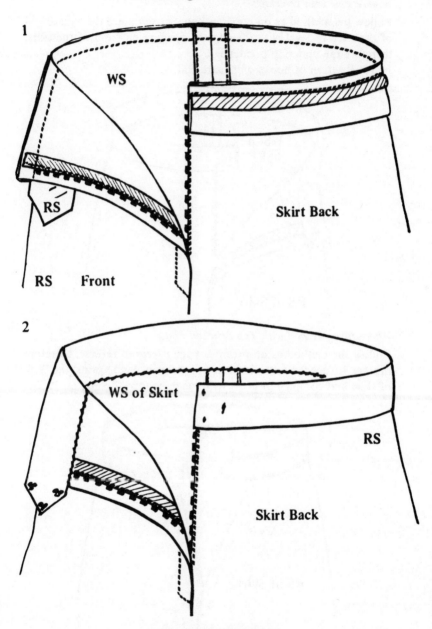

Waistband Completed

Dressmaking Simplified

Square End with Overlap:

Follow the method as on previous page, *except* place the square end of the overlap level with the edge of opening on front of the skirt, therefore the underlap is extended.

NOTE: Position of hooks on square end.

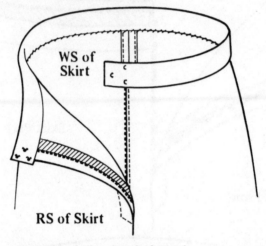

Alternative Method with Top Stitched Finish

Follow the method as on previous page *except* in reverse, therefore in stage 1 place the unstiffened side of the waistband against the W.S. of skirt and complete process with machine top stitching on R.S.

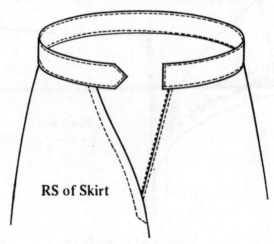

Petersham Bands

As the petersham is not seen from the R.S. it is suitable for skirts with decorative style lines such as hip yokes. It is particularly useful for finishing the waistline of bulky tweed fabrics. Petersham is available not only in plain black or white but also with spaced bones, for added support, and also with one slightly looser edge for use on hipster skirts and trousers.

Preparing the Petersham

1. Cut the length required, i.e. firm waist measurement plus 2·5 cm for ease plus 2·5 om for neatening.
2. Turn back 1·25 cm at each end and hem the raw edges.
3. Attach two hooks and eyes. Method for attaching page 158.

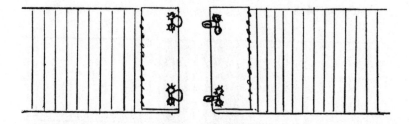

4. Neaten the raw edges and base of fastenings with straight binding. Hem into position.
5. Divide band into four sections and mark with a tack line.

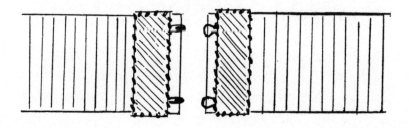

Dressmaking Simplified

Setting in petersham for waistline with edge to edge fastening

1. Turn garment through to W.S. and divide waist edge into four sections and tack mark.
2. With R.S. of petersham over W.S. of skirt bring the edge of petersham to waist fitting line. Place each end of petersham level with edges of opening.
3. Matching the quarter section marks, pin and tack edge of petersham to fitting line, easing in skirt if necessary (see diagram below).
4. Machine stitch edge of petersham. Remove tacks and press.
5. Trim raw edges to 1 cm and neaten on R.S. with a straight binding hemmed on to the stitched line and then flat on to petersham enclosing raw edge (Diagram 1 opposite).
6. Turn band down on to W.S. of garment and press (Diagram 2 opposite). The hooks and bars now face in towards the skirt, in this position they are easier to fasten and prevented from catching into underwear.

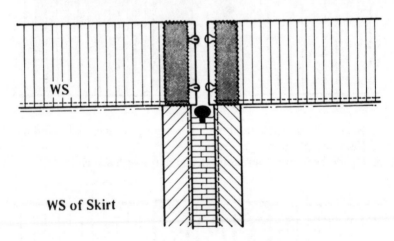

WS

WS of Skirt

1.

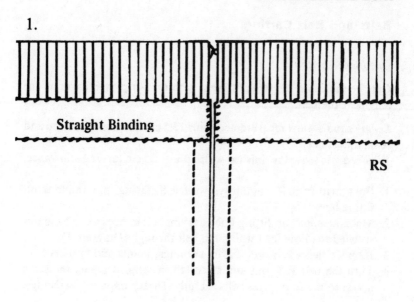

Straight Binding

RS

2.

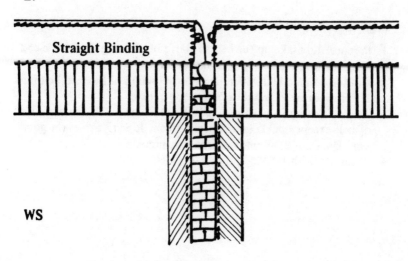

Straight Binding

WS

Dressmaking Simplified

Belts and Belt Carriers

Unstiffened belts

Cut the fabric on the straight grain with the warp threads along the length of the belt.

Length equals waist measurement plus 12·5 cm for ease, overwrap and seam allowance.
Width equals twice the finished width plus 1·25 cm turning allowance.

1. Fold strip in half lengthways with R.S. facing, pin and tack on fitting line.
2. Machine stitch on fitting lines, leaving a gap approx. 7·5 cm unstitched to allow for turning the belt through (Diagram 1).
3. Remove tacks and press. Trim turnings, points and corners.
4. Turn the belt R.S. out and slipstitch the gap. Bringing the seam up on to the fold, press belt carefully. Attach required fastenings.

NOTE: Long tie belts are made in the same way but cut to the required length.

Stiffened belts

1. Prepare and make up the belt as above but leaving the buckle end open for turning through (Diagram 2).
2. Cut the bonded belt stiffening the exact width of finished belt but 2·5 cm shorter in length to allow for buckle.
3. Tack stiffening in position on W.S. Machine stitch around edge of belt except buckle end, working from R.S. to achieve a good line (Diagram 2). Remove tacks and press.
4. Complete with buckle and metal eyelets.

1. **Unstiffened Belt or Tie**

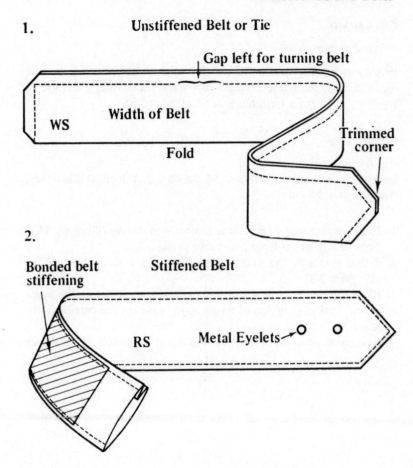

Gap left for turning belt

WS   Width of Belt

Fold

Trimmed corner

2. **Stiffened Belt**

Bonded belt stiffening

RS   Metal Eyelets

Belt Carriers

Worked carrier

Work a straight loop stitched bar the width of belt plus 0·6 cm, sew on to the side seam above and below waist seam, follow method of working given for a buttonhole loop on page 150.

Fabric carrier

Cut fabric on straight thread.
Length equals width of belt plus 0·6 cm plus 2 cm turning allowance.
Width equals 2·5 cm.

1. Fold the two long edges to the centre, W.S. facing (Diagram 3A). Fold in half again lengthways and press.
2. Either slipstitch the folded edge or machine stitch both edges (Diagram 3B).
3. Place the carrier centrally over the side seam and across the waist seam. Tack in position allowing slight ease on the carrier (Diagram 3C).
4. Sew securely in place with hemming or backstitch as shown in Diagram 3C.

Belt Carriers

3.

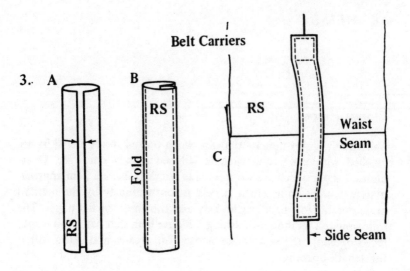

18 HEMS

Blouse Hems

Shirt blouses and blouses that are worn tucked inside the skirt are finished with a narrow machine stitched hem 1 cm wide. Over-blouses, those which are worn outside the skirt, have a hem approximately 3–4 cm wide which is held inconspicuously by the method most suitable for the fabric and style as shown on earlier pages. The following is a method of finishing a blouse hem that has a full length faced opening: the same finish is used for dresses and skirts with a full length opening.

1. Fold the facings with raw edges neatened on to the R.S. of the blouse and machine stitch across the base of the facing along the fitting line.
2. Trim the turnings of the facing to 0·6 cm below the machine stitching. Trim across the corners of both the blouse and the facing (Diagram 1).
3. Fold back the facings on to the W.S., ease out the corners and press.
4. With the R.S. of the blouse flat on the table, fold the hem up on to the W.S. along the fitting line and prepare the hem as given on page 202- 203.
5. Slip hem the fold into position and oversew the facing to the hem (Diagram 2). Remove the tackings and press.

Blouse Hem with Faced Opening

1.

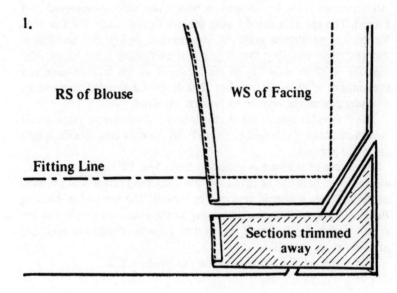

RS of Blouse

WS of Facing

Fitting Line

Sections trimmed away

2.

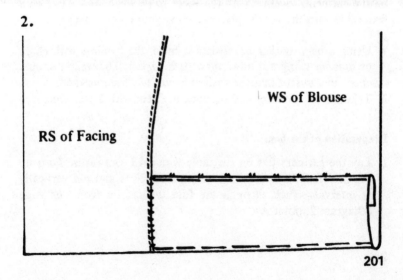

RS of Facing

WS of Blouse

Hems

All processes must be completed before the hem is measured and turned. The garment should hang for two days to allow the fabric to 'drop', i.e. to stretch with its own weight, *before* the hemline is marked, thus ensuring that it remains even after completion. The amount of 'drop' depends on the looseness of the fabric weave and the amount of 'flare' in the skirt. The drop of a circular skirt can be considerable as the true cross grain is involved.

The finished length of the skirt is influenced by current fashion and is either a particular height or depth from the knee or a specific length from the ground.

The depth of the hem is generally from 5 to 7·5 cm: on children's wear a 10 cm hem can be made to allow for letting down with growth; on thin fabrics a double hem can be turned. The method of holding the hem in position varies according to the fabric and style and the most suitable finish should be selected. Details of different methods are shown on page 204.

The stitching of a hem should be invisible on R.S.

To mark the hem

The assistance of a second person is essential as the hemline is measured *up* from the floor with the help of a hem marker or yard-stick held in a vertical position (Diagram 1). The wearer should put on the garment, together with the shoes to be worn, and stand on a firm table with the weight placed evenly between both feet.

1. Using a hem marker or yardstick, mark the hemline with chalk or pins, marking not more than 10 cm apart. The wearer should check in a mirror that the desired length has been marked.
2. Take off the garment and re-mark the hem with a tack-line.

Preparation of the hem

1. Lay the garment flat on the table with W.S. outwards. Turn up the hem from the tack line, match seam lines and pin vertically at intervals. Tack through the fold 0·6 cm up from the edge (Diagram 2, point A).

2. With a marker card or tape measure mark the depth of the finished hem with a horizontal line of pins or with tacking taken through the *single* fabric only (Diagram 2, point B).
3. Trim away surplus fabric, leaving a 0·6 cm turning allowance beyond the marked line (Diagram 2). Complete the hem as is most suitable (see page 204). Diagram 3 shows a slip hemming worked in alternative manner to that shown on page 69.

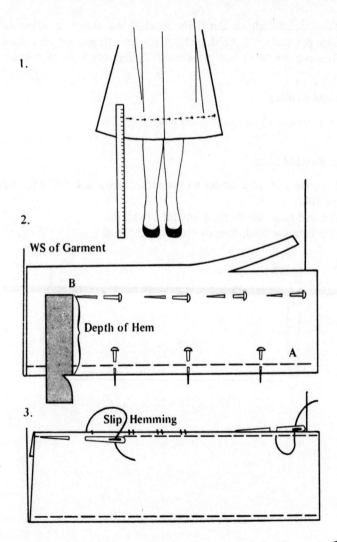

1.

2.

WS of Garment

B

Depth of Hem

A

3. Slip Hemming

Straight Hemlines: finishes

First match and pin seam lines, then the sections between seams.

Slip hemming: shown on pages 69 and 203

For general use on lightweight fabrics.

1. Turn the raw edge under to the marked line, then tack in position.
2. Slip the hem, the fold picking up one thread of R.S. fabric. Remove the tacks and press carefully from R.S. in each case.

Straight Binding

See the diagram and method on page 208.

Edge Stitched Hem

1. Turn the raw edge under to the tacked line, tack and edge stitch the fold.
2. Pin and tack the stitched line into position.
3. Slip hem the fold. Remove tacks and press.

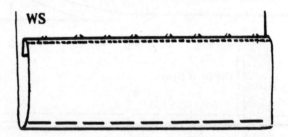

Bound Hem

Suitable for thick fabrics that fray easily. Using silk or fine nainsook, bind the raw edge of hem, following the method for binding given on page 110 and complete as for an edge stitched hem.

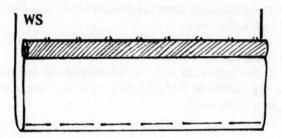

Herringbone Edge

Suitable for thick fabrics.

1. Trim turnings to marked line, i.e. the width of hem. Pin and tack into position.
2. Work herringbone stitch, picking up one thread on the R.S. of fabric and stitch normally on the hem turning.
3. Remove tacks and press.

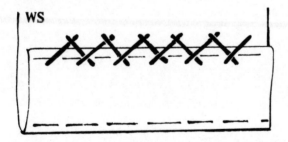

Dressmaking Simplified

Circular Hemlines: finishes

The hem is usually 0·6 cm deep as otherwise there would be too much fullness to disperse owing to the width of the flare.

1. Measure 0·6 cm down from the marked hemline and turn hem to W.S. on this line: tack.
2. Edge stitch along the fold and trim away the surplus fabric: then press (Diagram 1).
3. Turn up the hem on to W.S. on the marked line and tack.
4. Either edge stitch the fold (Diagram 2), or slip hem stitched fold into place (Diagram 3).

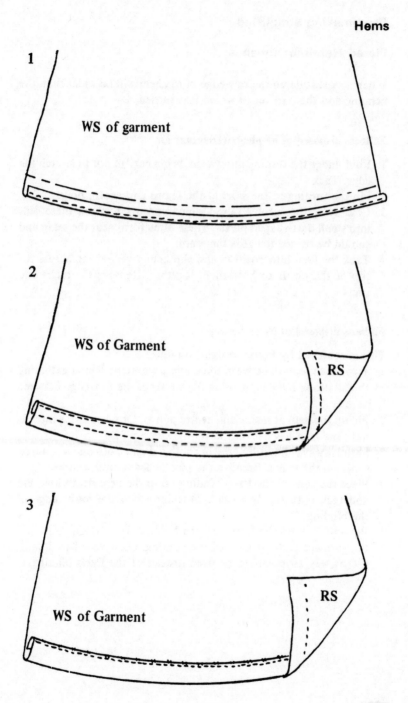

1

WS of garment

2

WS of Garment

RS

3

WS of Garment

RS

Flared Hemline: finishes

When a skirt is flared the raw edge of the hem will be wider than the hemline and the part on to which it is turned.

Fullness disposed of by pleats (Diagram 1).

1. Fold under the turning allowance, being careful not to stretch the edge. Tack.
2. Pin the turning to the skirt at the seams and centre points.
3. Fold away the surplus fabric which appears between these pins into small dart-shaped pleats. These often form near the seam and should be turned towards the seam.
4. Tack the hem into position and slip hem, over-sewing across the top of the pleats to hold them together. Remove the tacks and press.

Fullness disposed of by gathering

This is neatened by Paris (straight) binding.
1. Treat each section between the seams separately. Run a gathering thread along the hem turning 0·6 cm from the raw edge between seams.
2. Pin up the hem at seams and centre points. Draw up these threads until the hem lies flat on the skirt (Diagram 2).
3. Shrink away fullness by pressing with a damp cloth and a hot iron (only on the edge). Remove the pins at seams and centres.
4. Place the edge of the Paris binding up to the hem depth line. Pin and tack it to the *hem* only. Machine stitch the lower edge of the binding.
5. Pin and tack up the hem with the binding flat and slip hem into the garment and flat edge of the binding. On a very flared skirt, a crossway strip should be used instead of the Paris binding.

Flared Hemlines

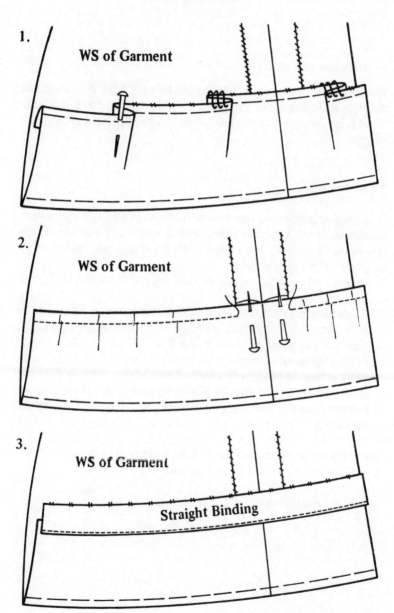

1. WS of Garment

2. WS of Garment

3. WS of Garment

   Straight Binding

19 DECORATIVE FINISHES

The method of decoration must be suitable for both the fabric and the style and purpose of the garment. If the garment is to be laundered it is essential that the decoration can be laundered in the same manner.

Shell Edging

A method of making narrow decorative hems or tucks on underwear, blouses and young children's wear that is made of soft or fine fabrics that do not fray badly. Use a firm silk or cotton thread without fluff to give a crisp appearance.

1. Turn a narrow hem, not more than 0·6 cm on to the W.S., and tack.
2. Work from the right to left on the W.S., fastening on with a double back stitch on to the hem. Pick up three running stitches in the hem without going through to the R.S.
3. Taking the needle over the fold, pass from the R.S. through to the W.S. at base of hem, work a second oversewing stitch in the same place and pull up tightly to pinch the hem. Take three running stitches into the hem only and repeat to finish hem. (Diagram opposite.)

NOTE: Space between the double tight stitches should not be more than 1 cm to achieve the correct pinched effect.

Alternative method: as used for tucks, see page 84.

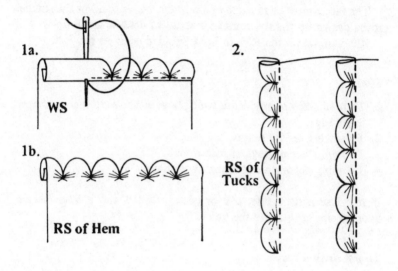

Pin Stitch

A decorative stitch for use on lingerie, children's wear and fine blouses.

The fabric must be fine and of a resilient weave to allow the stitches to be drawn up tightly to make a series of definite small holes.

It is worked on the R.S. to hold a folded edge on the R.S.

Uses:

1. To hold hems of any width which have either a straight *or* shaped inner edge.
2. To stitch overlaid seams.
3. To apply lace edgings or insertions.
4. To apply decorative sections of appliqué.

NOTE: Use a firm, fine, silk or cotton thread and a large needle, average size 6, to make the holes.

To pin stitch a hem

1. Turn the hem up on to R.S. and tack in position. The first fold should be evenly trimmed to not more than 0·3 cm.
2. With fold towards the worker, work from right to left, fastening thread with a double stitch in the fold.
   (i) Take a small straight stitch into the single fabric below the fold (Diagram 1a).
   (ii) Repeat this stitch using precisely the same holes and draw up tightly (Diagram 1b).
   (iii) Place needle again into first hole and bring it out into the hem directly above the second hole, and in a square position (Diagram 1c).
   Repeat from stage (i) placing the needle precisely into the last hole of double stitch (Diagram 1a).

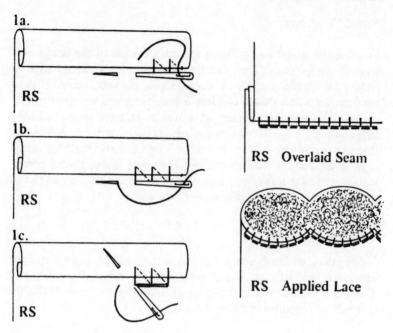

1a.

RS

1b.

RS

1c.

RS

RS   Overlaid Seam

RS   Applied Lace

213

Faced Scallops

Faced scallops are used to form the main feature of the design and style of the garment. They can be placed to give a shaped edge to collars or necklines, cuffs or sleeve edges, pockets, openings, and hemlines on women's and children's underwear and top garments.

Faced scallops are worked in a similar manner to an ordinary shaped facing page 120, therefore all seams must be completed so that the facing can be carried out in a continuous length or circle.

In order that all scallops are of a complete shape, i.e. no partial scallop, the edge must first be measured to determine the number of scallops and the necessary diameter and width.

To make a template

Having decided the diameter (width) of the scallops, draw a straight line on a strip of card and draw a line of circles of the required diameter. Accurately cut the scallops following the curved edge on one side of central line (shaped area).

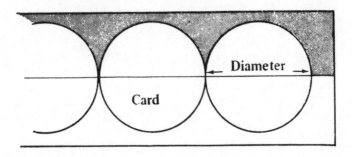

To mark the scallops on to the garment

Place the card template exactly in position on the W.S. with the outer edge of the curves against the fitting line and hold firmly in place. Using a sharp piece of tailor's chalk, carefully draw around the edge of the scallops.

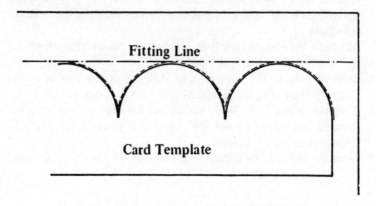

Fitting Line

Card Template

To face the scallops

1. Join facing as necessary and neaten the inner raw edge: see page 120.
2. Place R.S. of facing R.S. of garment, matching balance marks and fitting lines exactly: pin and tack into position. Using small stitches tack round the marked line. If the facing is slippery, upright tack the facing in position before tackling the scallops (Diagram 1).
3. Machine the curved tack line, making the points sharp between the scallops. Remove tacks and press.
4. Trim turning to 0·6 cm and snip into the points almost to the stitching; snip diagonally against the curves (Diagram 2).
5. Turn the facing to the W.S., easing out the scallops and bring the stitched line up on to the fold; tack into position (Diagram 3). Press lightly under a cloth.
6. Hem the edge of the facing to the turning of the seam (see page 121).

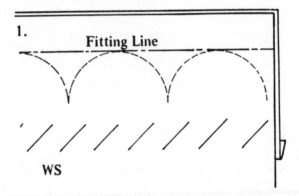

2.

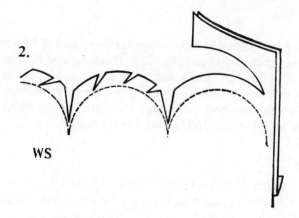

WS

3.

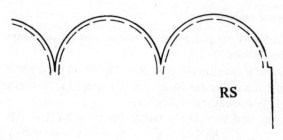

RS

4.

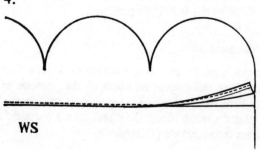

WS

Faggoting

Faggoting is a method of linking together two pieces of fabric with a decorative stitch to give an open finish. It can be used to attach lace or frills to a hem, to make a decorative seam or, with the use of a rouleau, to form an open work edging or decorative insertion.

The illustrations show the use of a rouleau but the method is the same for applying lace, frills or for making a seam.

Rouleau

This is a length of crossway fabric sewn to form a long tube which can then be used for faggoting as shown, for the insertion of patterns or for buttonhole loops: see page 152. As it is made from crossway fabric, it is very flexible and adapts readily to a curved position.

To prepare a rouleau

1. Cut crossway strip 2·5 cm wide and join if necessary for the required length.
2. Fold in half lengthways with R.S. facing. With a loose tension, machine stitch through the centre (Diagram 1a): the loose tension makes the rouleau more flexible.
3. Trim one end to a sharp point, thread a bodkin with a short double thread looped through the eye and sew securely to the end of the tube.
4. Push the bodkin into the tube (Diagram 1b) and gently ease the rouleau through the R.S. (Diagram 1c).

To prepare the garment

Neaten the raw edge by the most suitable method, either by a self-binding or a false bind equal in width to the rouleau *or* a shaped facing *or* on firm fabrics by turning a narrow fold to the W.S. and working a running stitch along the edge; turn a second fold 0·6 cm wide and press into position (Diagram 2).

Preparation and method of faggoting

1. On a narrow length of strong paper draw two parallel lines 0·6 cm apart.

2. Tack the edge of the garment against one line and tack the *stitched* edge of the rouleau against the second line (Diagram 3).

NOTE: The distance between the lines can vary according to the fabric and the choice of stitches.

3. Using a firm silk or cotton thread without fluff, fasten on into the fold of the rouleau and work stitching as shown on page 220. Maintain an even tension for a good finish.

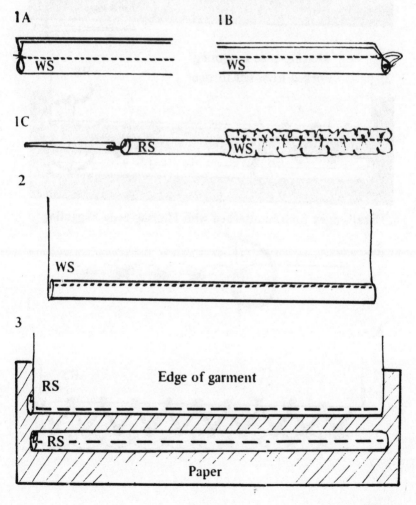

1A

WS

1B

WS

1C

RS   WS

2

WS

3

RS

Edge of garment

RS

Paper

Faggoting Stitches

1. **Bar Faggoting worked from right to left**

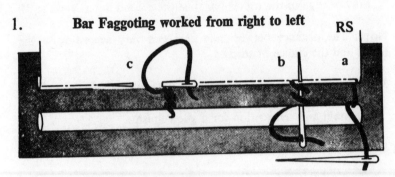

2. **Herring-bone Faggoting worked from left to right**

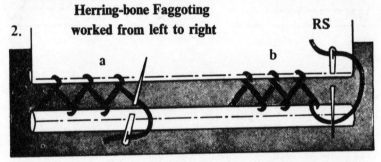

Shell-edged rouleau attached with Herring-bone Faggoting

3.

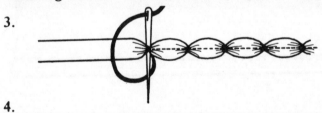

4.

Frills

Frills are applied either for decoration or to lengthen a garment. The amount of fabric depends upon the desired effect.

Slight fullness: the required length plus half as much again.
Average fullness: twice the required length.
Very full frill: three times the required length (of fine fabric only).

To prepare a frill

1. With the warp threads running the length of the frill cut the length or lengths required plus turnings by the finished width plus turnings.
2. Join the lengths with a plain seam.
3. Complete the hem of the frill.
4. Work a line of gathering threads either side of the stitching line.

Lace frills: an allowance as for fabric frills. A draw thread for gathering is usually to be found on the straight edge. Lace can be inset by any of the given methods.

Ready-made frilling: purchase the required length plus turnings only and inset by any of the following methods.

Method of setting in frills

Overlaid seam (Diagram on page 222): Draw up the frill to the required length and make an overlaid seam (page 102) with the garment section overlaid on to the frill.

With a decorative band (diagram on page 223): Draw up the frill and join to the garment with a plain seam (page 95) made with the W.S. facing so that turnings are on the R.S. Press the garment up from the stitching against the turnings. Hem the decorative band to the frill immediately below the stitched line on R.S. and sew the second side flat on to the garment with hemming or a decorative stitch, thus enclosing the raw edges.

Inserting a frill into a panel line (Diagram 3 on page 223): Draw up the frill and tack into position on the fitting line on the R.S. of the under section. Prepare the upper section and make an overlaid seam (page 102); thus enclosing the edge of the frill.

Setting in a frill with a shaped facing (Diagram 4 on page 224): Join facing and neaten the outer edge. Draw up the frill and tack into position on the fitting line on R.S. of garment. Place the R.S. of facing over the frill and matching fitting lines, tack and stitch. Complete as for a shaped facing (page 120).

Frills

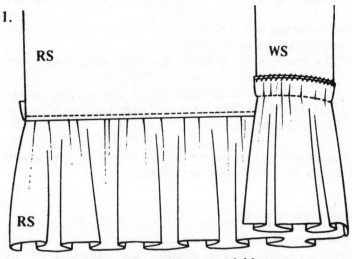

1.

RS   WS

RS

Frill attached with an overlaid seam

2.

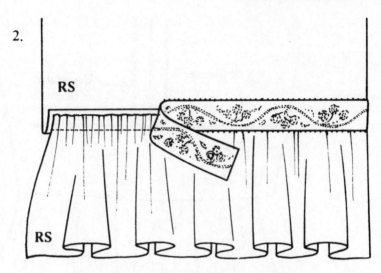

Raw edges neatened by lace or ribbon

Frills

3

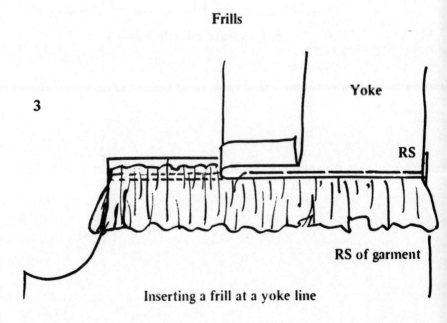

Inserting a frill at a yoke line

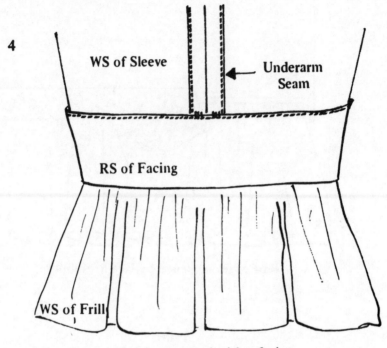

4

WS of Sleeve

Underarm
Seam

RS of Facing

WS of Frill

A frill neatened with a facing

Lace

For joining lace use the finest thread available that is suitable for the colour and texture of the lace. For applying lace use a firm silk or cotton thread that does not fluff but which handles and looks well.

Narrow lace edging

To join

1. Match the pattern by overlaying the two layers exactly; the effect will otherwise be blurred.
2. Closely oversew around the corded edge of the design to completely join the lace (Diagram 1 on page 227).
3. Trim away the raw edges close to the stitching on both R.S. or W.S.

To shape

If less than 1·25 cm wide, ease the lace into position: if more than 1·25 cm wide used without gathers, it is necessary to make small darts at corner point.
1. For the central angle of brassiere top slip sew a small dart with its point going into the angle (Diagram 2 at A).
2. For the shoulder strap point reverse the placing of the point (Diagram 2 at B).
3. On the W.S. flatten the dart and hem on to the back of the lace (Diagram 2).

Alternate methods of attachment

1. Oversewing the edge closely to the garment and trimming away the surplus fabric: this is not suitable for gathered lace.
2. Overlay the lace on to a narrow folded hem and machine stitch (Diagram 2).
3. Overlay the fabric on to the lace and make an overlaid seam.
4. Oversew the lace to the edge of a triple-folded hem (Diagram 1).

Wide lace, shaped insertions and piece lace

The repeat of the design may be too large to allow for the pattern to meet exactly: the same method is used to both join and shape the lace.

1. Mark the fitting lines on the lace and overlap the sections so that the fitting lines match.
2. Select and mark the best continuous outline of the lace that passes across the fitting line.
3. Oversew very closely on marked line and trim off surplus lace.

To attach

Either over-sew (satin stitch) or pinstitch the edge of the lace on to the garment, trimming away any surplus fabric (Diagram 3a and b). On piece lace *do not* make a hem but utilize the finished edge of the lace.

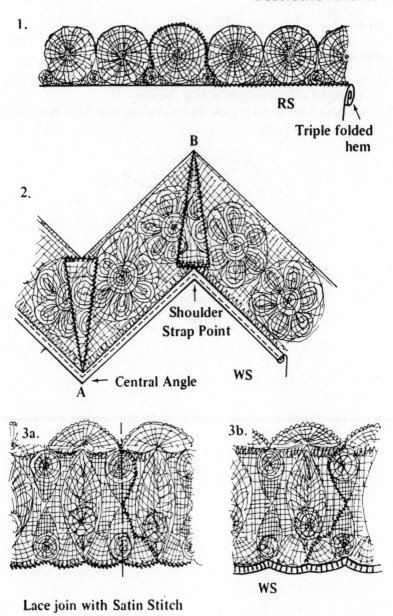

1.

RS

Triple folded
hem

2.

B

Shoulder
Strap Point

Central Angle

A

WS

3a.

3b.

WS

Lace join with Satin Stitch

Braid

Flat braid

1. Tack the braid flat into position, making small mitred seams at the angles and joining the ends if necessary.
2. Machine stitch or backstitch the braid along each edge. Remove the tacks and press.

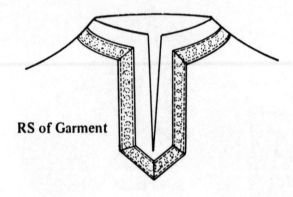

RS of Garment

Military braid and braid used as binding

On single fabric trim off allowance for turnings.

By hand: guide the braid on equally over the edge and tack through the layers. Stab stitch along the edge of the braid from the R.S. through to W.S.

By machine: Open out the braid and tack into position on R.S. with $\frac{1}{2}''$ width of braid projecting from the edge. Machine stitch along edge of the braid. Turn the projected edge over on to the W.S. and hem on to the machine stitching.

Corners: Wide corners can be negotiated by stretching the middle of the braid and easing the edges.

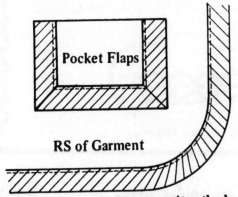

On right-angled and shaped corners, mitre the braid on each side and oversew edges together

Decorative Stitches

Interlaced Back-stitch

Double Interlaced Back-stitch

Pekinese

Whipped Back-stitch

Double Whipped Back-stitch

Feather Stitch

Chain Stitch

Stem Stitch

20 CARE AND MAINTENANCE OF CLOTHES

To maintain the good appearance and obtain the most wear out of a garment, it is essential to take good day-to-day care of the garment and to repair at the earliest signs of wear.

General Rules

1. After use, brush outer garments and place on a hanger so that the creases drop out naturally. In the case of jumpers and knitted dresses, fold neatly and store in a drawer. Allow clothes to air overnight before storing.
2. Remove all brooches or pins before putting the garment away.
3. Try not to wear the same dress or skirt on consecutive days so that the fibres regain their original shape.
4. Check regularly that no seam is coming unstitched or that a button is loose. A button lost often means that a complete set has to be bought as it is difficult, after a period, to match up.
5. Do not put perfume on to a garment as it may stain the fabric: it will also go stale quickly.
6. Check for moth. Do not store clothes that are damp or in a damp place.
7. Remove spots as soon as possible.
8. Read the maker's label for special washing or cleaning instructions before laundering.
9. Never let the garment become too soiled before washing or cleaning as heavy laundering damages the fibres and if dry cleaned the ingrained dirt will remain.

Hedge Tear Darn

Whenever possible the darning should be worked with threads of the same fabric so that the repair is less conspicuous.
Following the diagrams opposite:

1. Working on the W.S. draw the edges of the tear gently together with fishbone stitch, using a very fine silk or cotton thread (Diagram 1 a and b).
2. Mark the 'L' shape of the darn with a tack line (Diagram 2).
3. Using the darning thread, work one side of the darn as far as the angle (Diagram 2).
4. Work the second side of the darn completely (Diagram 3) starting at point A.
5. Complete the first side. The weakest point of the tear is then supported by double darning (Diagram 4).

Hedge Tear Darn

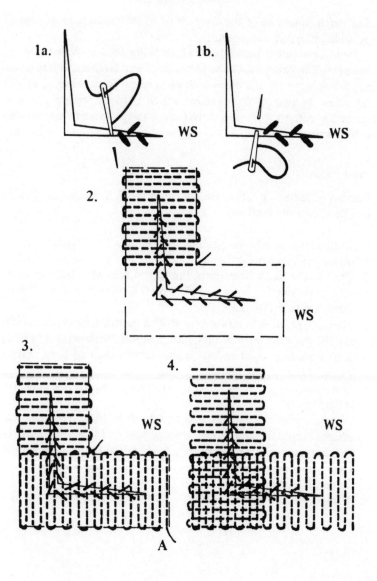

Patching

The patch should be of the same fabric as the garment or as near as possible in texture and colour.

New fabric must be washed before being used to repair a worn garment. The patch should be rectangular and large enough to cover any fabric worn around the hole. It must be cut from the same way of fabric as the part of the garment which is to be repaired, and in matching pattern lines check that the straight threads are parallel before sewing.

Print Patch

Patches of patterned fabric are put on to the R.S. so that the design can be accurately matched.

1. Outline the area to be patched, including all the worn area, by tacking (Diagram 1a).
2. Cut out the patch, the size of the tacked area plus 1·25 cm turnings, matching the pattern. Fold over 0·6 cm turnings on all four sides and tack (Diagram 1b).
3. Place the patch R.S. upwards to R.S. of garment, carefully matching the pattern; pin and tack into position. With printed fabrics, it is more important to match the pattern than to keep exactly by the thread of the fabric.
4. Over-sew into position all the way round; remove the tackings (Diagram 2).
5. Flatten the work carefully and turn to W.S. Make two diagonal creases across the hole from corner to corner. Place a pin 1·25 cm in from the corners on each crease. From the hole cut up on the crease lines to the pins then cut across the straight of the fabric from pin to pin.
6. Neaten the raw edges together with loop stitches (Diagram 3).

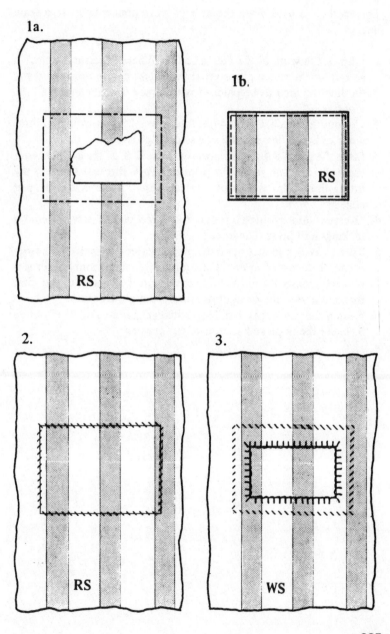

Patch into a seam

This method is used when the hole or worn area extends to a seam line.

1. Unpick the seam in the area affected. Where necessary remove a section of the sleeve also so that the patch may set into the seam. Outline the area to be patched with a tack line, including all the worn area.
2. Cut out the patch. On the W.S. fold over 1·25 cm turning on three sides and tack, leaving the side seam edge free.
3. Place the patch R.S. uppermost on to the R.S. of the garment over the hole. Pin and tack into position. Tack through to mark the fitting line. Trim any surplus fabric which overlaps the garment edge.
4. Oversew into position around the three tacked sides. Remove tackings and press (Diagram 1).
5. Turn to W.S. and make two diagonal creases across the hole, from corner to corner of sewing. Place a pin 1·25 cm in from the corners on each crease. From the hole, cut up on the creases to the pins, then cut across the straight of fabric from pin to pin.
6. Neaten the raw edges with loop stitch (Diagram 2).
7. Remake the unpicked section of the garment.

Patch into a Seam

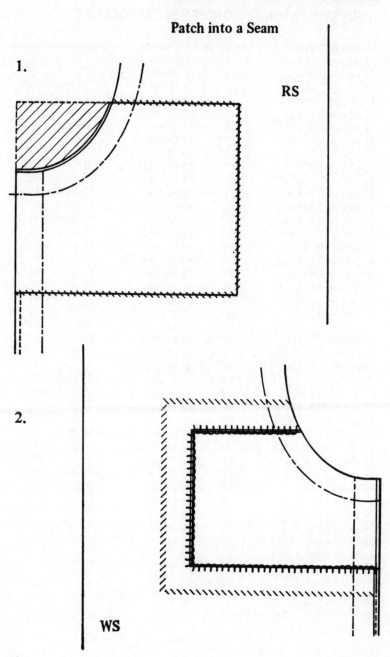

1.

RS

2.

WS

MEASUREMENT CONVERSION TABLES

Yards to Metres

$\frac{1}{4}$ yd	= ·229 m
$\frac{1}{2}$ yd	= ·457 m
$\frac{3}{4}$ yd	= ·686 m
1 yd	= ·914 m
$1\frac{1}{4}$ yds	= 1·143 m
$1\frac{1}{2}$ yds	= 1·372 m
$1\frac{3}{4}$ yds	= 1.60 m
2 yds	= 1·82 m
$2\frac{1}{4}$ yds	= 2·058 m
$2\frac{1}{2}$ yds	= 2·286 m
$2\frac{3}{4}$ yds	= 2·515 m
3 yds	= 2·743 m
$3\frac{1}{4}$ yds	= 2·972 m
$3\frac{1}{2}$ yds	= 3·20 m
$3\frac{3}{4}$ yds	= 3·429 m
4 yds	= 3·558 m
$4\frac{1}{4}$ yds	= 3·887 m
$4\frac{1}{2}$ yds	= 4·115 m
$4\frac{3}{4}$ yds	= 4·344 m
5 yds	= 4·572 m

Metres to Yards

$\frac{1}{4}$ m =	$9\frac{7}{8}''$
$\frac{1}{2}$ m =	$19\frac{5}{8}''$
$\frac{3}{4}$ m =	$29\frac{1}{2}''$
1 m =	1 yd $3\frac{3}{8}''$
$1\frac{1}{4}$ m =	1 yd $13\frac{3}{4}''$
$1\frac{1}{2}$ m =	1 yd $23''$
$1\frac{3}{4}$ m =	1 yd $32''$
2 m =	2 yds $6\frac{1}{4}''$
$2\frac{1}{4}$ m =	2 yds $16\frac{5}{8}''$
$2\frac{1}{2}$ m =	2 yds $26\frac{3}{8}''$
$2\frac{3}{4}$ m =	3 yds $\frac{1}{4}''$
3 m =	3 yds $10\frac{1}{8}''$
$3\frac{1}{4}$ m =	3 yds $20''$
$3\frac{1}{2}$ m =	3 yds $29\frac{3}{4}''$
$3\frac{3}{4}$ m =	4 yds $3\frac{5}{8}''$
4 m =	4 yds $13\frac{1}{2}''$
$4\frac{1}{4}$ m =	4 yds $23\frac{3}{8}''$
$4\frac{1}{2}$ m =	4 yds $33\frac{1}{8}''$
$4\frac{3}{4}$ m =	5 yds $7''$
5 m =	5 yds $13\frac{7}{8}''$

Inches to Centimetres

$1''$ =	2·54 cm
$2''$ =	5·08 cm
$3''$ =	7·62 cm
$4''$ =	10·16 cm
$5''$ =	12·70 cm
$6''$ =	15·24 cm
$7''$ =	17·78 cm
$8''$ =	20·32 cm
$9''$ =	22·86 cm
$10''$ =	25·4 cm
$11''$ =	27·94 cm
$12''$ =	30·48 cm
$13''$ =	33·02 cm
$14''$ =	35·56 cm
$15''$ =	38·1 cm
$16''$ =	40·64 cm
$17''$ =	43·18 cm
$18''$ =	45·72 cm
$19''$ =	48·26 cm
$20''$ =	50·8 cm
$21''$ =	53·34 cm
$22''$ =	55·88 cm
$23''$ =	58·42 cm
$24''$ =	60·96 cm
$25''$ =	63·5 cm
$26''$ =	66·04 cm
$27''$ =	68·58 cm
$28''$ =	71·12 cm
$29''$ =	73·66 cm
$30''$ =	76·2 cm
$31''$ =	78·74 cm
$32''$ =	81·28 cm
$33''$ =	83·82 cm
$34''$ =	86·36 cm
$35''$ =	88·9 cm
$36''$ =	91·44 cm
$37''$ =	93·98 cm
$38''$ =	96·52 cm
$39''$ =	99·06 cm
$40''$ =	101·6 cm

Centimetres to Inches

1 cm =	$\frac{3}{8}''$
2 cm =	$\frac{3}{4}''$
3 cm =	$1\frac{1}{8}''$
4 cm =	$1\frac{1}{2}''$
5 cm =	$1\frac{7}{8}''$
6 cm =	$2\frac{3}{8}''$
7 cm =	$2\frac{3}{4}''$
8 cm =	$3\frac{1}{8}''$
9 cm =	$3\frac{1}{2}''$
10 cm =	$3\frac{7}{8}''$
11 cm =	$4\frac{1}{4}''$
12 cm =	$4\frac{5}{8}''$
13 cm =	$5''$
14 cm =	$5\frac{3}{8}''$
15 cm =	$5\frac{3}{4}''$
16 cm =	$6\frac{1}{4}''$
17 cm =	$6\frac{5}{8}''$
18 cm =	$7''$
19 cm =	$7\frac{3}{8}''$
20 cm =	$7\frac{3}{4}''$
25 cm =	$9\frac{5}{8}''$
30 cm =	$11\frac{3}{4}''$
35 cm =	$13\frac{5}{8}''$
40 cm =	$15\frac{3}{4}''$
45 cm =	$17\frac{3}{4}''$
50 cm =	$19\frac{5}{8}''$
55 cm =	$21\frac{5}{8}''$
60 cm =	$23\frac{1}{8}''$
65 cm =	$25\frac{5}{8}''$
70 cm =	$27\frac{1}{4}''$
75 cm =	$29\frac{3}{4}''$
80 cm =	$31\frac{1}{2}''$
85 cm =	$33\frac{1}{2}''$
90 cm =	$35\frac{1}{4}''$
95 cm =	$37\frac{3}{8}''$
100 cm =	$39\frac{1}{4}''$

Table of Suggested Fabrics for Everyday Garments

Garment	Lightweight		Medium		Heavyweight	
Blouse	Cheesecloth	C.	Calico	C.P.	Sailcloth	C.P.
Shirts	Lawn	C.P.	Cambric	C.	Fine wool Angora	W.
Tops	Georgette	C.S.P.	Crepe du Chine	S.	Wool Jersey	W.
	Muslin	C.P.	Dimity	C.		
	Nainsook	C.	Gingham	C.P.		
	Organdie	C.P.	Pique	C.P.		
	Voile	C.P.	Poplin	C.P.		
			Seersucker	C.P.N.		
			Tussah	S.		
			Viyella	W.		
Beachwear	Cheesecloth	C.	Gingham	C.P.	Terry Towelling	C.
	Lawn	C.P.	Helanca	P.		
	Jersey	C.P.	Poplin	C.		
			Stretch Towelling	P.N.		
Nightwear	Lawn	C.P.	Brushed Rayon	R.	Flannelette ⎱ Flame	C.
	Jersey	C.P.N.	Dimity	C.	Wincyette ⎰ proof	
			Poplin	C.		
			Seersucker	C.N.		
Dresses	Cheesecloth	C.	Brocade	S.R.	Angora	W.
	Lawn	C.P.	Brushed Fabric	C.P.R.	Boucle	W.S.
	Nainsook	C.	Corduroy	C.P.	Flannel	W.
	Poplin	C.P.	Courtelle	P.	Grograin	S.R.
	Sarille	R.	Crimplene	P.	Tweed	W.P.
	Tricel	R.	Jersey	C.S.W.P.N.	Velvet	S.P.
	Tussah	S.	Orlon	A.		
			Sailcloth	C.P.		
			Velvet	C.P.R.		
			Velveteen	C.P.		
			Viyella	W.		
Jackets	Courtelle	A.	Boucle	W.	Barathea	W.
Skirts	Jersey	C.W.P.N.	Corduroy	C.P.	Cavalry Twill	W.N.P.
Trousers	Orlon	A.	Denim	C.P.	Donegal Tweed	W.
	Pann Velvet	P.	Drill	C.	Drill	C.W.
	Treveira	P.	Sailcloth	C.	Flannel	W.P.
			Velvet	C.P.R.	Fur	A.
			Velveteen	C.P.	Gaberdine	W.P.
			Velour	C.		

Key
C. – Cotton
W. – Wool
S. – Silk
P. – Polyesters
R. – Rayon
N. – Polyamides (Nylon group)
A. – Acrylic